THE PROJE
MANAGER'S POCKET
SURVIVAL GUIDE

James P. Lewis

McGraw-Hill
New York   Chicago   San Francisco
Lisbon   London   Madrid   Mexico City
Milan New Delhi   San Juan   Seoul
Singapore   Sydney   Toronto

The *McGraw·Hill* Companies

1 2 3 4 5 6 7 8 9 0 AGM/AGM 0 9 8 7 6 5 4 3

ISBN 0-07-141621-8

PMP, PMI, and PMBOK are registered trademarks of the Project Management Institute.

McGraw-Hill books are available at special quantity discounts to use as premiums and sales promotions, or for use in corporate training programs. For more information, please write to the Director of Special Sales, McGraw-Hill, Professional Publishing, 2 Penn Plaza, New York, NY 10121-2298. Or contact your local bookstore.

This publication is designed to provide accurate and authoritative information in regard to the subject matter covered. It is sold with the understanding that neither the author nor the publisher is engaged in rendering legal, accounting, or other professional service. If legal advice or other expert assistance is required, the services of a competent professional should be sought.
—*From a Declaration of Principles jointly adopted by a Committee of the American Bar Association and a Committee of Publishers.*

This book is printed on recycled, acid-free paper containing a minimum of 50% recycled de-inked fiber.

Dedicated to The Chieftains
For 40 years of music projects that have
enriched the lives of so many

And to the memory of Derek Bell
1929–2002

Contents

List of Figures

Preface

In this time of economic turmoil, survival is the order of the day. Companies routinely try every "program of the month" that promises to improve the bottom line. They have downsized, rightsized, wrongsized—and some have capsized. So to say that jobs are also precarious is an understatement.

There is one thing certain: If you aren't better than the competitors for your job, one of them will get it, and you will be in the job market. The question is: what does it take to be just 10 percent better than everyone else? How do you protect your job from the piranha who circle at the first sign of blood, eager to consume you in a feeding frenzy of job competition?

The Project Manager's Pocket Survival Guide proposes to answer these questions, to give you an edge on the piranha, so that you survive and thrive in this turbulent time. I have drawn on my own experience as a project manager for some 15 years in the industry, combined with 22 years of training and consulting to companies on project management, plus the experience of some of my colleagues, who have shared their insights in this book.

Of course, there are no guarantees. There is always a matter of luck. You can be in the right place at the right time, the wrong place at the wrong time, and all the other permutations of these statements. However, bad luck may cost you your job; seldom does good luck get you a job. That usually requires some skill on your part.

As always, when I write a book, I encourage my readers to let me hear from them. So you will find my e-mail address at the end of this preface. Since I travel extensively, I may be a bit slow answering, but I will try to answer all e-mails from readers. You may also want to visit my web site periodically to see what resources have been placed there, as we try to make the site a resource to my readers as well. The URL is www.lewisinstitute.com.

In any case, thank you for buying my book and good luck with your career.

Jim Lewis
Vinton, Virginia
April 2003
e-mail: jlewis@lewisinstitute.com

Acknowledgments

I *want to thank several individuals* for contributing to this book. Janet Atkinson, PMP, has been a longtime supporter of my work, and she has a good on-the-job perspective of project management. Barry Briggs set up my second web site and maintains it. He has very keen insight into real-world projects. Bob Dudley, PMP, spent 30 years in the trenches doing projects, and is one of my certified instructors. George Hollins, PMP, was initially a client but is now a good friend and avid supporter of project management. Alan Mulally, President and CEO of Boeing Commercial Airplanes, has been a supporter for several years. My book, *Working Together,* describes his principles for managing. I do believe those principles are the key to success in managing projects as well.

As usual, my wife, Lea Ann, has read the manuscript and added art that enhances the text and keeps it lively. As she is always at the end of the chain in my book projects, she is also the victim of the common project situation in which all of the float (and then some) has been used up before the work reaches her, so that she is working to an impossible deadline.

Lora Hansen takes my wife's concepts and polishes them on the computer to produce the final illustrations. And Judy Brown then typesets the entire job. My wife, Lora, and Judy have now worked on three books together, so I think we can be called a team.

Finally, Catherine Dassopolous, my acquisitions editor at McGraw-Hill, has always been an enthusiastic supporter of my project management books, and I greatly appreciate her support.

As we writers say, these contributions have made the book better. Any shortcomings are my own.

1

It's a Jungle Out There!

S*ome years ago,* a project manager was given the assignment to refurbish a large processing line in a mill. It was a huge job, with most of the cost being in capital equipment. He and his team worked on estimating the cost to do the job, then presented the $60 million estimate to the company president. The president suffered a stroke on the spot.

When he recovered, he yelled, "Sixty million! The last job like this only cost thirty million! How can it be so high?"

The project manager tried to explain that many things were different between the two jobs, that the former job was several years past and costs had escalated significantly since then, but the president would hear none of it. "You have to be able to do it for less," he insisted.

It's a jungle out there!

Do It Better
Do It Faster
Do It Cheaper

Finally, the project manager agreed to do the best he could to keep the cost down. When the job was finished, the cost was $62 million. That was only 3 percent above his original estimate—but it was 32 million more than the president thought it could be done for. The president responded by firing the project manager. Fortunately for the project manager, he quickly got a job at another company in town—as a vice president!

This is certainly an extreme example, but not entirely an unusual one. In the past 25 years, I have heard many similar stories. As my friend, Doug DeCarlo, says, "It's a jungle out there!" And to survive the jungle you must know the ways of the jungle. That's what this book is about—how to survive and thrive in the jungle—as a project manager!

PROJECT FAILURES

In 1996, the Standish group conducted a study revealing that about 85 percent of all information systems (IS) projects get into trouble, failing to meet their performance, cost, time, and scope targets. This means that they are late, overspent, have reduced functionality, and so on. In fact, the situation was so bad that 33 percent of such projects had to be canceled altogether. Of the $250 billion spent on software projects, this means that nearly $80 billion was just thrown away.

Surely, the situation is better today, you say. I'm afraid not. Studies continue to show high rates of failure, with one estimate indicating that we wasted $128 billion on software projects in 2001.

Well, it must be that those software people are dummies. It *can't* be that bad in other areas. Maybe not; maybe construction projects are better.

The truth is, product development projects of all kinds have high failure rates, and the same is true of R&D (research and development) projects. It's just that more studies are being conducted on software projects, so we see the numbers, whereas studies are lacking in other areas.

Now you are presumably reading this book because you manage some kind of projects, and you would like to survive in the jungle. In that jungle, companies of all kinds are demanding that projects be done better, faster, cheaper—with fewer resources ("do more with less," they say). They have downsized, rightsized, wrongsized (or capsized), all in an effort to cut costs and boost profits.

On top of that, the workforce is changing. Many of the managers who attend my seminars lament that the work ethic is a thing of the past. Many of their younger team members seem to think that if they show up for work, that's all that should be expected of them. In addition, the managers to whom project managers report seem to be more and more demanding, with some having a "win at all costs" attitude. Others adopt an extreme, "no excuses" position in response to any problems encountered in a project. How do you survive as a project manager in such a climate? Or maybe we should ask, how do you *succeed*?

I don't know how many project managers are fired because their projects fail to meet targets. I really don't believe it is that many. However, I do believe that the stress generated in the minds of all parties is quite high, and that the cost to our society is far greater than just the costs of project overruns—costs such as stress-related illnesses, problems away from work with one's spouse and family, and so on. Not to mention the fact that people leave jobs when confronted with impossible situations, so that their lives are uprooted, careers disrupted, and dreams dashed.

Many problems with projects stem from factors totally outside the control of project managers. Merger mania may have diminished somewhat, but it is still a factor. I know of one organization that bought a division of another company, and that division took over a project currently being managed by an existing division of the parent company. The project manager was displaced (or demoted—depending on how you look at it), the project was stalled while the newly acquired company tried to find out what was going on to begin with, and people were laid off for economic reasons.

> *Not all successful managers are competent and not all failed managers are incompetent. Luck still plays a part in success or failure, but luck favors the competent, hardworking manager.*
>
> — Rule 10, from NASA, 1996

My guess is that most—not a few, but *most*—companies are pursuing far more projects than they have adequate resources to staff. As I have shown in my other books (Lewis, 2000, 2001), this leads to constantly shifting priorities, as one project gets into trouble and must be rescued by robbing resources from another, the overall result being work that starts and stops, increasing setup time and contributing to significant productivity loss. One company found that prioritizing projects so that each person had a first-priority job, with a backup, nearly doubled productivity! That reflects the high cost of setup time.

Survival Tip: It's bad enough to be late and overspent, so be sure the deliverable is what it is supposed to be!

Interestingly, as Graham et al. (2003) have written, if a project produces a winning outcome, the cost overruns are forgotten. If it fails to deliver, then the cost overruns are the subject of much lamenting, fingerpointing, and recrimination.

Forecasting & estimating are both guessing.

Every weather forecast carries a probability factor.

Project estimates often have no history.

THE FIRST MYTH

The truth of the matter is that we are sometimes victims of the very methodology that is supposed to make our projects succeed. We are supposed to use a work breakdown structure to identify all work that must be done and to develop estimates for task durations, resource requirements, and costs. Then a critical path schedule is produced (a PERT diagram, to use popular language). Now we know how long the project will take, and we can control the work using earned value analysis to measure progress.

There is a fundamental problem with all this, though. It has to do with estimating. As I write these words it is snowing. The forecast started by predicting—several days ago—that we would probably get an inch of snow. Then it changed almost hourly until last night. In the end, we will know the facts only after the snowfall ceases.

Here's my point: forecasting and estimating are both *guessing!* That's right. Meteorologists measure wind direction, speed, and temperature. They watch cloud formations. They examine weather history. And they apply "laws" that state if warm air and cold air collide, you can expect something to happen. It may snow. There may be a tornado. Or your pigs may suddenly decide they don't like mud. Heck, we don't know for sure!

> **Survival Tip:** Never give a sponsor a range on an estimate. Give him a not-to-exceed. If you give him a range, he will remember the low end, you will remember the high end, and . . .

But at least meteorologists are honest. They tell us, point blank, that the weather *may* act as they predict. *Every* forecast carries with it a *probability!*

Project estimating (forecasting) is different. If we have done something before, that becomes the basis of our estimate. As an example, if I ask you how long it takes you to get to work every day, you might say, "Typically, it takes about 30 minutes. The best I've ever done is 25 minutes, and occasionally it takes 45." Now wait a minute. What is this "typically" and "about" nonsense? As your manager, I want you to tell me how long it will take you to get to work tomorrow—*exactly* how long. "I can't do it," you say.

"Why not?"

"Well, there are too many factors outside my control," you reply. "I can only tell you about how long it will take."

"Okay, so how long is that?"

"Well, make it 35 minutes," you say, nudging it up a little from the typical time because my pressure on you is making you a bit uneasy.

"Okay, 35 minutes it is," I say, making a note in my personal digital assistant (PDA)—and making you wish you had just gone for broke and told me 45 minutes instead. After all, it's never taken longer than that. And because I entered it into my PDA, you know I am going to hold you to it. You also know that I have deleted that qualifier "about" from what you have just told me. What I have heard is that it will take you 35 minutes to get to work, no more and no less. Suddenly, your probabilistic number has become deterministic—that is, exact! You are in trouble before you start, unless you are clever enough to get to work early, drive around the building several times, until it is exactly 35 minutes since you left home, and, with great fanfare, drive jubilantly into the parking lot *exactly on time!*

As your manager, I am impressed. You have proven that if I manage you correctly, I will get the results I expect. And you have confirmed that the project management seminar that I paid for you to attend, together with that great software, Microsoft Project®, that I gave you, have both paid off. Isn't life wonderful?

The very tools that are supposed to help us succeed with projects actually create an *illusion of precision* that does not exist. All estimates are probabilistic, because all activities vary. There is "noise" in every process that makes every process variable. Statisticians have shown this in manufacturing processes

"Exact estimate" is an oxymoron!

for many years, and have taught us how to plot control charts so we can see the range of variation involved, thus enabling us to tell when the process is running *normally* and when it is *out of control!* We understand that improving the process reduces the variation, but it can never be eliminated. Yet we forget this when we look at other processes—such as doing project work.

If we can just get everyone to recognize this fact—so that they think statistically, rather than deterministically—we would have much less grief in organizations, and we would all suffer much less stress. I am convinced, however, that this is not likely to happen in my lifetime, so we will have to find other ways to deal with reality.

THE PLACE TO BEGIN

If you are serious about being a project manager for the next few years, and you don't want to be a casualty of some of the jungle forces mentioned above, then the place to begin is with yourself. You have to know the laws of the jungle to survive, and most of us do not come equipped for this. Furthermore, you need survival skills. School never gave you any of them, so you will have to develop them on your own. (You learned math, but did they

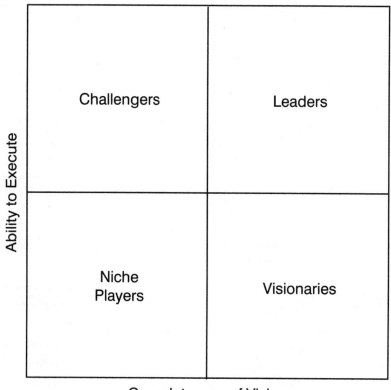

Figure 1.1
The Gartner Grid

teach you to balance your checkbook? Or create a budget? Or calculate the interest on a credit card?) At best, we leave school with a diploma that should certify us as jungle dummies, not jungle survivors.

The Gartner Grid

In 1999, the Gartner Group developed a two-dimensional grid to look at software products. I believe it can be applied to organizations and individuals equally well. It is shown in Figure 1.1.

The two dimensions on the grid are *completeness of vision* and *ability to execute*. When an individual, company, or product rates low on both dimensions, you have a niche player. This might characterize the novice project manager. By increasing your ability to execute, but not your vision, you become a challenger. By increasing your vision but not your ability, you become a visionary but not yet a real player. The person who rates high on both dimensions is the true leader, which is what each of us should aspire to be.

Completeness of Vision

Completeness of vision means that you have a clear visualization of a world-class project manager (see Wysocki & Lewis, 2000, for more on this). You know the skills and attributes required to be world class. You can see him in your mind's eye. You can hear him speak, and you know what he would say. You can predict his every move—how he would react to various situations, the posture he would adopt.

Ability to Execute

But can you play the part? Can you emulate the world-class project manager? Vision without ability to execute is not going to get results. Ability to execute without vision will yield a partial solution. You must have both. You must hone your skills. You must develop the ability, the same way you would approach being a world-class athlete. You train, practice, play the game, get feedback, train more vigorously, and go at it again.

> *If there is nothing very special about your work, no matter how hard you apply yourself, you won't get noticed, and that increasingly means you won't get paid much either.*
>
> — Michael Goldhaber, *Wired*
> (Quoted by Tom Peters in a speech)

THE MISSING PUZZLE PIECE

Schools don't teach us life skills. As I said previously, when you get a diploma, it should cite you as a jungle dummy, not a jungle survivor. Many, if not most, of us go through life never knowing

Many of us go through life never knowing the laws that govern living.

———

Nevertheless, we face the consequences.

the laws that govern living. Ignorance of a law does not make you immune from the consequences of breaking it. Thus, it is important that we know what governs life.

A law is a cause-effect relationship. If you do A, then B will result. Did you ever have a Laws of Life course in school? I doubt it.

Let me tell you about education first-hand. After spending nearly 15 years in engineering, I decided to get a doctorate in psychology because I had learned that knowing how to deal effectively with people was the number one skill a manager needs. Now, don't you go and sign up for a Ph.D. program yet, because I'm not finished with the story.

I earned my Ph.D. in 1986, when I was 45 years old. However, I had finished all the course work and taken my exams in 1980, so all that remained was to do my dissertation. In May 1981, I started teaching seminars on "Leadership Skills for Project Managers," sharing my newfound academic knowledge combined with my in-the-trenches experiences with people. It was pretty good stuff, and I enjoyed it. But then a recession hit, and I learned a hard lesson. Companies don't value training very much when they are hurting economically, and the least valued of all training is "soft-skills" training. My work dropped to nothing overnight.

My next move was fortuitous. I bought a personal computer, because it became clear to me that this was the coming thing, and besides that, I'm an engineer at heart, so I love high-tech toys. When the fellow who ran the agency I worked with learned that I had some computer skills, he asked if I could teach a seminar on project management and the personal computer. I could. I didn't know what the heck it meant, but I was sure I could do it. I put together a program on creating spreadsheets for use in projects, along with creating project schedules. (Initially, this was with VisiCalc and VisiSchedule.)

We packed them in. My calendar was full for the next three years, until I burned out teaching the same course day after day. What to do now?

I knew there was little use trying to revive the old leadership course, but I had learned that one weakness in my computer course students was that they knew very little about project management. I was convinced, however, that they now had some powerful tools that would allow them to mess up their projects, big time. That meant the only thing to do was teach them about project management.

When I started teaching, Harold Kerzner and I both worked for the same agency as contract instructors. There were probably a half-dozen of us in the entire United States teaching project management. We were ahead of the curve. It started to turn up around 1991, and peaked about 1998 or so.

Now, you may think I have digressed, but I have not. From about 1991 until 1998, I taught about 1,000 people annually how to manage projects. Or I thought I did, anyway. Then I had a realization: Many people who had attended my seminars had the *tools* of project management, but still did not know how to use them. They still thought like technologists, or accountants, or whatever their education had made them, but they didn't think like managers. Some of them couldn't manage themselves, let alone other people. I don't mean this to be disparaging—my point is, I trained them inadequately.

Knowing what the tools are without knowing how to use them is useless. Remember the Gartner grid—ability without vision is not the way, nor is vision without ability. You must have both.

I had given them ability without vision.

Now, for the climax to my story.

I also knew that a major failing has been that companies won't pay for soft-skills training. They see no bottom-line correlation with soft skills. Well, to understand the blindness of this position, think about how many projects you have seen fail because the project manager didn't know how to create a solid schedule. And how many have you seen self-destruct because of "people problems?" People in conflict, not listening to each other, not cooperating, not collaborating. Lack of motivation and commitment. You name it, that's the big source of trouble.

Daniel Goleman, in his book *Primal Leadership* (2002), has confirmed that there is a bottom-line payoff when leaders possess high emotional intelligence, which has to do with how a person handles himself and his relationships. They report the following findings in a study of a large accounting firm:

> *If the partner had significant strengths in the self-management competencies, he or she added 78 percent more incremental profit than did a partner without those strengths. Likewise, the added profits for partners with strengths in social skills were 110 percent greater, and those with strengths in the self-management competencies added a whopping 390 percent incremental profit— in this case, $1,465,000 more per year.*
>
> *By contrast, significant strengths in analytic reasoning abilities added just 50 percent more profit. Thus, purely cognitive abilities help— but the EI competencies help far more (Goleman, et al, 2002, p. 251).*

There are four major components to EI: self-awareness, self-management, social awareness, and relationship management. Each of these, in turn, consists of a number of subcomponents. Since I have covered these in my book *Project Leadership* (2002), I won't go into detail about them. The point I want to make is that we are finally learning the importance of the soft skills. Without these, you are left with a highly skilled robot, with no heart or soul, trying to manage people.

Applying the Theory

I mentioned that I hold a Ph.D. in psychology. That must mean that I know how to deal with people pretty well and how to manage myself—right?

Wrong.

Nowhere in my psychology program was I taught anything about living. I know all kinds of things about how teams function, about effective leadership and communication, but none of it goes to the core of everyday living with people. Maybe I should soften that a little. I did have all of the theoretical underpinnings. I do know the basic causes of human behavior. I know something of people's mental processes. But nowhere did I learn the *practical application* of the theory!

Along Came Phil

There was a popular song in the 50s or 60s called "Along Came Jones"—slow-walking, slow-talking Jones. I am reminded of it when I think of a book by Dr. Phillip McGraw, which came out in 1999, called *Life Strategies: Doing What Works, Doing What Matters*. I saw it on the shelves immediately, because I can't pass a bookstore without stopping. I didn't buy it, because it was a bestseller and I have learned to be very suspicious of pop psychology books. So many of them are pablum that, if we could feed babies with them literally, we could end world hunger in children.

The thing is, that book has stayed on the shelves ever since it was released. So one day, my curiosity got the better of me. If nothing else, I thought I would peruse it just so I could throw rocks at this pop psychologist. To my surprise, I found myself agreeing with him—and furthermore, I began to see how to apply all that theory that I learned in school! Incredible. Being an engineer, I have great disdain for knowledge that can't be applied, so for years I have been annoyed at my own education.

My life didn't get much better after I got my Ph.D., nor did my ability to deal more effectively with people. I say "much" because there was definitely some benefit, but far less than I expected.

PROJECTS ARE PEOPLE!

Find out what makes people tick.

———

Create your own experience of the jungle.

The Ten Laws of Life

In his book, Dr. Phil presents ten laws of life and explains how to apply them to improving your life. I am going to list them here, along with a brief comment about how I think they apply to project managers. I encourage you to read Dr. Phil's book in its entirety when you get a chance.

1. You either get it or you don't. Applied to project management, this means that if you don't understand people and what makes them tick, you are likely to fail, because *projects are people!*

2. You create your own experience. Since this is a survival guide, and this chapter addresses the jungle out there, it would be easy to cop out and blame the jungle for all your problems as a manager. You can't do that. The jungle will place obstacles in your way: it is how you respond to them that matters. You create your own experience of the jungle. Many years ago, I read about a

man and wife who were having marital difficulties. Dr. Milton Erickson sent each of them to visit the botanical gardens in Phoenix. The man came back saying he had a wonderful experience at the gardens. His wife was bored to death. Same gardens, different experience.

3. People do what works. The point of this law is that we continue to do those things for which we receive a pay-off. The payoff may not always be pleasant, but it is better than the alternative. If there is no payoff, you will quit behaving in a certain way. Any time you experience problems with people on your team, ask what pay-offs they are getting that cause them to behave as they are, and you will have the key to dealing with them.

4. You cannot change what you do not acknowledge. This one is pretty obvious. As a project manager, you can't handle project problems—whether they have to do with the work itself or the members of your team—unless you acknowledge that the problems exist. And you certainly can't solve a problem that you yourself are causing unless you acknowledge your own culpability.

5. Life rewards action. We often have the intention to take certain steps in our lives or our jobs, but we just never get around to it. Intentions don't resolve issues or solve problems. Only action can do so. Resolve to be a person of action rather than one of good intentions.

6. There is no reality; only perception. You may have to reflect on this one in depth to accept it, but remember the botanical gardens. The man labeled the gardens as beautiful. The woman labeled them boring. The gardens were neither. It was the *perception* of each that made them boring or beautiful. As Shakespeare wrote, there is nothing either good or bad but thinking makes it so.

7. Life is managed; it is not cured. There are no magic pills to cure your life or management problems. You must take charge and manage rather than look for a quick cure.

8. We teach people how to treat us. As a manager, if you feel that people on your team don't give you any respect,

ask yourself how you have taught them to behave toward you in this way. I have seen new managers approach teams in such a self-deprecating manner that it is impossible for people on the team to respect them. Have you inadvertently done the same?

9. There is power in forgiveness. Anger and resentment will kill you. We tend to ignore the mind-body relationship, but researchers have found that emotions cause chemicals to be generated in the brain and other parts of the body that either have a positive or negative effect upon it. Positive emotions cause chemicals to be secreted that result in positive effects, and vice versa. Forgive people for their injustices to you. Otherwise, you are doing *yourself* in, not them.

10. You have to name it before you can claim it. Get clear about what you want and you can achieve it. Going through life with fuzzy goals will yield a fuzzy life, whether as a manager or an individual. As the Gartner grid shows, you need a powerful vision, together with ability, in order to be a world-class project manager.

2

The Role of the Project Manager

*M*ost *of us become project managers accidentally.* We are in the right place at the right—or wrong—time, depending on your point of view. My friend, Bob Wysocki, calls us *accidental* project managers. A few individuals choose project management as a career move. These people Bob calls *deliberate* project managers. I have met some accidental project managers who would call deliberate project managers dumb, because in their view nobody with any sense at all would actually choose the profession. Nevertheless, the Project Management Institute now (as of April 2003) has over 100,000 members, and about 54,000 of them have received PMP® certification, meaning they have decided that project management is the profession that they want to pursue at this point in time.

Some of us are accidental project managers, and some of us are deliberate project managers.

Which one are you?

Many people actually manage projects without seeing themselves as project managers, or without being called project managers. Then there are individuals who manage projects but are not project managers. These people deal with what most people call one-person projects. I say these individuals are not project managers for a simple reason—to be a manager, you must have someone reporting to you, either on a solid-line or a dotted-line basis. I know, there are a lot of people who companies call managers who have no one reporting to them. I'm sorry, they aren't really managers. If they qualify as managers because they are managing themselves, then everyone in the building likewise qualifies to be called a manager. (Obviously, everyone does not hold my view; if you disagree, that's okay.)

> **Survival Tip:** Try very hard not to be a *working* project manager!

There is also a distinction to be made between the dedicated (or full-time) project manager and the part-time one. Often, part-time project managers are called *working* project managers. This is usually a euphemism for a person who is actually doing a lot of work and pretending to manage a job, because any time there is a conflict between getting work done and managing the project, you know which one takes priority. The net result is that the managing suffers. Furthermore, at performance appraisal time, the person's supervisor is likely to say: "Your work was fine, but your managing of the job left a lot to be desired." Being a working project manager is the kiss of death. If you find yourself in this trap, you definitely need this book. Read on.

The reason for this trap is that it is not yet widely recognized that managing projects is a *function,* just as are accounting, human resources, or engineering. We don't want everyone in the company doing his or her own accounting, so we hire people who have specialized skills in that area to do the accounting for us. But project management—that's a different matter. Everyone should be able to do that.

> **Survival Tip:** If you *are* a working project manager, don't let the work sidetrack you from the managing.

Unfortunately, there is a problem here that will make me seem to be contradicting myself. I believe everyone can benefit from knowing how to manage a project, even though they may not function as project managers. The reason is that managing a project is a disciplined way of thinking, and this thought process can be applied to any project—even one-person projects. As I said at the beginning of this chapter, you may be managing a project without being a project manager.

IF YOU ARE GOING TO BE A PROJECT MANAGER

If your career plan calls for you to be a project manager for some extended period, I want to say that the most important survival tip is to be a *competent* project manager. To be a competent project manager goes beyond just taking an introductory course in the subject. It also goes beyond getting your PMP®, the designation given by the Project Management Institute if you pass their certification exam and meet other requirements (see www.PMI.org for more details). The reason I say this is that the PMP exam will test your academic knowledge of the areas covered, but it will not teach you how to actually manage projects.

> **Survival Tip: Become a *competent* project manager!**

In fact, learning to manage is like becoming a star athlete. You don't learn to be an athlete by reading a book or attending a seminar. You learn through coaching, practicing, falling down, losing, getting up and starting over! You learn through the "school of hard knocks." If you're lucky, you have a coach or mentor who is able to help you get through the worst of it without receiving too many scars along the way. Still, *you* have to do most of the hard work. Your coach can only help you maximize your strengths and minimize your weaknesses.

We'll talk more about coaches and mentors later, but I strongly advise you to become active in PMI and network with other project managers if you are serious about project management as a career, at least for the next few years. Learn everything you can about the profession. Develop your skills, especially those having to do with people—such as negotiation skills, communication, group process, dealing with conflict, and so on. Remember, project management is a job that deals mostly with people. Technology is secondary.

WHAT IS MANAGING?

Managing has often been defined as "getting work done by other people." Very little thought is required to realize that this is hardly a satisfactory definition. Guards over prison work teams get work done by the prisoners, but is this managing? I don't think so. As far as I am concerned, Peter Drucker is the leading authority on managing, and he addressed this question in his book, *Management: Tasks, Responsibilities, Practices* (1973). Drucker states that a manager is expected to make an independent contribution to the success of the organization. In other words, a manager is expected to be a pro-active, rather than a reactive, contributor to the organization.

PROJECT MANAGEMENT DEFINED

I define project management as facilitation of the planning, scheduling, and controlling of all activities that must be performed to meet project objectives. Note the word *facilitation*. There is always a temptation to do the planning and scheduling yourself. If you do, though, you will most certainly shoot yourself in the foot.

There are two basic reasons. One is that people have very little commitment to a plan that they had no part in preparing. They know that the estimates you made are most likely not valid for them, and there are probably a number of flaws in your plan. Secondly, you can't possibly know how everything in a complex, multidisciplinary project should be done, so

> **Survival Tip:** The first rule of project planning is that the people who will do the work should plan that part of the project.

your plan will probably have some big holes in it. For these reasons, the first rule of project planning is that the people who will do the work should plan that part of the project.

Ultimately, your objective as project manager is to ensure that the project meets all objectives. These generally include performance, cost, time, and scope (or PCTS). *Performance* refers to what the "thing" produced is supposed to do. How is it supposed to perform? If it is a car you are designing, and it is supposed to get 25 miles per gasoline on the highway, does it do so? In other words, performance is generally spelled out in a user requirements document, product specification, or contract.

Cost refers to project costs. This is the so-called budget for project work. It includes materials, labor, and capital equipment. In some organizations, a dollar value is not assigned for the project budget, but you are given a certain number of people to do the

The project manager's job is to ensure that the project meets all objectives.

PERFORMANCE • COST • TIME • SCOPE

work, and this represents the labor component of your budget, even if no dollar figure is specified.

Time refers to the time frame for the project. In today's world, most projects are deadline-driven. The customer wants the job finished by a certain date, or marketing needs the new product by a certain date so they can begin selling it.

Scope refers to the work that must be done. If the company doing the project plans to do some work in house and contract out other components, then there will be a scope for both parts of the job. It is very important that scope be well defined. What *will not* be done is often more important to state clearly than what *will* be done. Otherwise, various stakeholders to the project may expect that you will do things you never planned to do, and will judge you harshly when they find you did not do as they expected.

One of the first survival techniques, then, is to have a firm agreement with all stakeholders to your project about exactly what each of these objectives means. And the most important thing to watch out for is having the project sponsor try to dictate

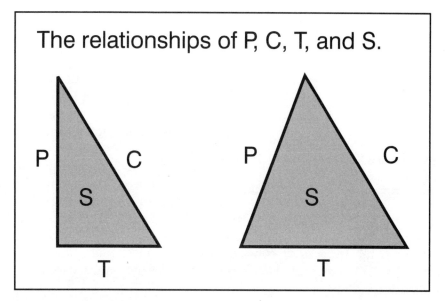

Figure 2.1
Triangle Showing Relationships of PCTS

values for all four objectives. Because these are interdependent, only three can actually be dictated. The fourth must be allowed to be determined by the nature of the job. An analogy is shown in Figure 2.1. If I know the values for the three sides of the triangle, the area (representing scope of work to be done) can be determined by a formula. Or, if I know the lengths of two sides and the area, I can calculate the length of the third side. But to arbitrarily assign values to all four of them is insane. If they actually work, it is an accident. (This is, in fact, one of the dozen or so most frequent causes of project failures.)

> **Survival Tip:** Get agreement with all stakeholders on PCTS targets.

Signatures

Although I generally dislike red tape and bureaucracy in projects, there is one area in which it is necessary. I said that you should be sure you have agreement with all stakeholders about the four targets. It is necessary, for everyone's protection, that this agreement be attested to: get everyone to sign off to the effect that they agree with the project plan, which will contain the specifications to be met, time frame, scope, and cost targets. Notice that all four are being specified. However, the sponsor gets to pick three of them and the project manager (together with his or her team) gets to "pick" the fourth one. This means, of course, that you will determine the value of the fourth one through the process of constructing the project plan. Once that number is specified, it also becomes a target that you try to hit.

> **Survival Tip: Agreement must be backed up with signatures.**

Expectations

It is possible to meet all four of the PCTS targets and still have people judge your project negatively. This is because all stakeholders have expectations for how the project will be managed—including things such as how often you communicate with them, what you tell them when you do communicate, how you treat them (with respect or disdain, for example), and many other factors. Failing to understand and manage stakeholder expectations can be a big mistake.

> **Survival Tip: Be clear about stakeholder expectations for your performance, and try to meet them.**

I once met some people who built and refurbished classrooms for a university. Midway through construction of a new building, the department that would occupy it got a new dean. When she walked through the new building, there were a number of things about it that she did not like. Had her issues not been addressed, the project could have been finished on time, budget, and scope, met all its performance requirements, and she would still have given the project a failing grade.

> **Survival Tip: Manage expectations.**

This is survival tip number two: be clear about customer expectations, negotiate when there is a difference between you and some stakeholder, and when a stakeholder changes, be sure to find out his or her expectations and manage them to conform to the ultimate plan.

IS MANAGING THE SAME AS LEADING?

Warren Bennis has written that we have too many managers and not enough leaders (2000). I heartily agree with him. As I wrote in the previous section, "to manage" is derived from a root that meant "to handle," and it has to do with the administration of budgets, schedules, and so on. To lead means to get others "to go along with." That is, a leader has followers. The best definition of leadership is one written by Vance Packard, and shown in the box to the side. The most important word in that definition is *want*. A leader gets people to want to do what must be done. A guard over a prison crew may get them to comply with directives, but the prisoners don't necessarily want to do so—the guard has a convincer called a gun. And many managers have a convincer called authority—the power to exercise sanctions over the employee who does not do what he or she is told to do. This is coercion, not leadership.

> *Leadership is the art of getting others to want to do something you are convinced should be done.*
>
> — Vance Packard

My personal belief is that we need somehow to instill in all managers the need to exercise leadership, and nowhere is this more important than in projects. The reason is simple—project managers often find themselves with a lot of responsibility and very little authority. That means that they must exercise influence to get things done. Unlike the manager to whom people actually report on a daily basis, the project manager has no ability to exercise sanctions over employees who refuse to do what they are told. So what can he or she do?

A great example came from a project manager who told me he took his nine-year-old daughter to a construction site one day. She was trying very hard to understand her father's job. What exactly did he do? She asked if all of the people she saw worked for him.

A project manager is a "tattletale."

He explained that they didn't work for him directly, but that some of them were working on his project. She then wanted to know if he told them what to do. He replied that he tried to influence them rather than just tell them.

"What do you do if they don't do it?" she asked.

"Well, I go talk with the person's boss," he explained.

Her face lit up. Suddenly she understood daddy's job. "Oh, you're a tattletale," she exclaimed gleefully.

So that's it. Now we know. A project manager is a tattletale!

Leadership is not a position. It is behavior. Leadership is granted by followers, not the organization!

Unfortunately, it is often true. When members of a project team don't report to the project manager, and won't do what must be done, then the only recourse is to talk with the person's direct supervisor and get that person to deal with the team member.

Clearly, if a project manager has strong leadership skills (translate that into good skills at persuasion and influence, among other things), there will be fewer situations in which an issue must be taken to another manager for resolution. That does not mean leadership is foolproof. There is always the possibility you have a "bad apple" on your team. But it is better to have 99 percent of your team follow you willingly than to have no followers at all.

> **Survival Tip:** Become a leader, not just a manager!

This all means, then, that you should work hard to develop your own leadership skills. And, yes, they can be developed. I have covered this subject extensively in my book, *Project Leadership* (Lewis, 2002), and it is outside the scope of this book to cover it again.

MINTZBERG'S ROLES[1]

Professor of Management at McGill University, Canada, Henry Mintzberg has written that: ". . . it is surprising how little study there has been of what managers actually do" (Mintzberg, 1989, p. 7). He goes on to say, "There has certainly been no shortage of material on what managers *should* do . . . Unfortunately, in the absence of any real understanding of managerial work, much of this advice has proved false and wasteful. How can anyone possibly prescribe change in a phenomenon so complex as managerial work without first having a deep comprehension of it?" (Mintzberg, 1989, p. 7).

To answer the question, Mintzberg shadowed a number of managers, meticulously recording what they do, how long they do it for, and with whom they do it. His findings are enlightening and certainly raise questions about the wisdom of the prescriptive material written by professors of management who have never managed.

The manager's job can best be described as a set of roles. These are organized sets of behaviors in which managers engage. Mintzberg has identified ten roles that fall into three categories.

Interpersonal Roles

I have often said that we sometimes think of project management as just scheduling. We forget that *projects are people,* and therefore dealing with people is one of the most important skill sets a project manager can possess. Mintzberg supports this in his findings about the interpersonal roles that a manager must play.

Figurehead

The first interpersonal role is the *figurehead.* By virtue of his or her position as head of an organizational unit, every manager must perform some ceremonial duties. These can include having lunch with important customers, attending weddings of employees, and

---

[1] Much of the material that follows was previously contained in my book, *Mastering Project Management* (Lewis, 1998).

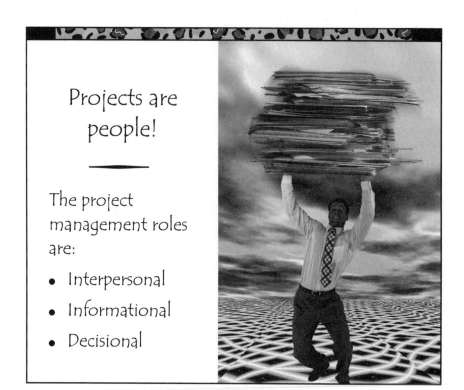

Projects are people!

The project management roles are:

- Interpersonal
- Informational
- Decisional

meeting with touring dignitaries. Some of these may seem trivial, but they are important to the smooth functioning of an organization and cannot be ignored by the manager. I would say that project managers have a certain number of these functions to carry out, so that this finding applies to project managers as well as to general managers.

Leader

Although I have discussed this above, here is what Mintzberg found about leadership. The manager must also perform the role of *leader*. Being in charge of an organizational unit, the manager is responsible for the work of the people in that unit. There may be both direct and indirect leadership roles to perform. Encouraging and motivating members of a project team would be a direct role in a pure project organization, and an indirect role in a matrix. As we have all heard so often, project managers usually have a lot of responsibility but little formal authority, so they must use influence to get things done. Leadership itself involves a great deal of influence activity, so it is one of the most important roles for the project manager.

Liaison

The third interpersonal role mentioned by Mintzberg is the *liaison*. This is a role in which a manager makes contacts outside of his or her vertical chain of command. There is no doubt that project managers engage in this role to a great extent. Some people call this the *boundary-crossing* role, because managers work outside the boundaries of their immediate unit. In fact, interfacing with people outside the unit is critical to the success of project teams. One of the major functions of such interfacing is to gather information. In effect, the liaison role is devoted to building up the manager's own external information system—informal, private, oral, but nevertheless effective.

Informational Roles

Through his interpersonal contacts, both with team members and with his network, the manager becomes the nerve center of his unit. He may not know everything, but he usually knows more than any one of his team members. Mintzberg found that managers spend nearly 40 percent of their contact time on activities devoted to the transmission of information. To a great extent, communication is the work of a manager.

Monitor

As a *monitor*, the manager is always scanning the environment for information. Much of the information that the manager receives is in oral form and consists of gossip, hearsay, and speculation. This soft information can be very important in alerting the manager to problems before they occur.

Disseminator

Managers must *disseminate* information, or it is of no use to the team. This is one area in which some managers fail, because realizing that information is power, they try to keep it to themselves.

The net result is that decisions cannot be made effectively by other members of the team, but must be made by the manager. Our favorite expression for this is that such a manager is a "mushroom" manager: he keeps people in the dark, feeds them a lot of nonsense, and when they grow up, he cuts them off at the knees and cans them.

Spokesperson

The *spokesperson* role is one in which managers pass information to people outside their units. This includes making presentations to higher-ranking managers, military officers in defense contracting projects, and sometimes to stockholders who are concerned about a major project.

Decisional Roles

Information is the basic input to decision making. Since the manager usually has more information than any single team member, he or she often plays a major role in making project decisions. Mintzberg has identified four decisional roles that the manager must perform.

Entrepreneur

The *entrepreneur* role is that of trying to improve the unit. In the monitor role, the manager is constantly on the lookout for good ideas. When she finds one, she may initiate a development project—this is the entrepreneur role. Even project managers may occasionally play this role, suggesting projects to senior managers. This would be especially true of technical project managers, who think of applications for technology and suggest new product development projects. We also find some corporations doing new business development projects, so that the project manager must play the entrepreneurial role to the hilt.

Disturbance Handler

Another decisional role is that of *disturbance handler*. Managers are initiators in the entrepreneurial role. In the disturbance handler

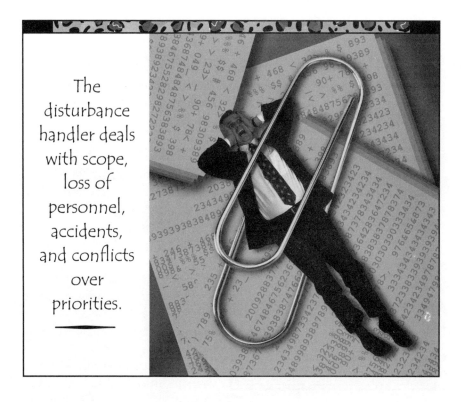

The disturbance handler deals with scope, loss of personnel, accidents, and conflicts over priorities.

role, they are reacting to pressures in which change is outside their control. For the project manager, this can take the form of changes in scope, accidents, loss of key personnel, and conflicts with functional managers over priorities.

Resource Allocator

The *resource allocator* role might be more the domain of the functional manager than the project manager, but even project managers have responsibility for deciding who will get what in the project team. One of the most important resources that the manager allocates is his or her own time. Access to a manager exposes the person to the team's nerve center and decision-maker.

Negotiator

Finally, we have the role of *negotiator*. There can be no question of the importance of this role to project managers. Together with the leader role, this is the way to get things done when you have no authority. Managers at all levels spend considerable time in negotiations, but negotiation is a *way of life* for the project manager.

The Integrated Job

It is important to stress that the ten roles described by Mintzberg are not separable. They form a *gestalt,* an integrated whole. This does not mean that all managers pay equal attention to all ten roles. The function that the manager performs will dictate that more time be given to one role than the others; however, you cannot neglect any one of them completely in any given management job.

> **Survival Tip: You can't be good at everything. Assess yourself. For those roles at which you are not very good, enlist the help of a team member.**

The fact that they do form an integrated whole is one reason for the difficulties of managing teams. "Two or three people cannot share a single managerial position unless they can act as one entity. That means they cannot divide up the ten roles unless they can very carefully reintegrate them" (Mintzberg, 1989, p. 22). The biggest problem is with the informational role. Unless there is full sharing of managerial information, team management breaks down. Since this is nearly impossible to achieve, we naturally can expect some problems with teams.

Prescriptions Based on Reality

It has often been said that to be effective we must understand ourselves. Insight into management work is a step in that direction. Success depends on how well managers understand and respond to the pressures and dilemmas of the job. Mintzberg has suggested three specific areas of concern for managers. I believe all of these apply to project managers.

1. *The project manager must find systematic ways to share his or her privileged information.* This can be done through regular debriefing sessions with key team members, by

maintaining a diary of important information for limited circulation, or by a memory dump to a dictating machine. To the degree that key team members have better information, they can make many of the decisions that would otherwise have to be made by the project manager. In her book, *Leadership and the New Science,* Margaret Wheatley (2001) has written that information is self-organizing, and that teams can benefit greatly by having the same information that the manager has at his or her disposal.

> **Survival Tip:** Keep all stakeholders informed about what is going on—especially your team members!

2. *The project manager must avoid pressures that would lead to superficiality by devoting attention to issues that require it, by looking at the big picture, and by making use of analytical data.* This boils down to knowing what is and is not a priority, so that you don't spend as much time on the trivial many as you do on the vital few. Members of the team have time to deal with the analysis of project status. The project manager must take full advantage of what these people have to offer and act on it appropriately.

> **Survival Tip:** Be clear on what constitutes a high-priority task, and focus on doing it.

3. *Project managers must gain control of their own time by turning obligations into advantages and by turning those things that they must to do into obligations.* Many things that managers are obligated to do could be considered just a waste of time. The effective manager makes the obligation into something positive. For example, a presentation can become an opportunity to lobby

> **Survival Tip:** Turn obligations into positives!

for resources for the team. A visit to a customer might be a chance to actually gain more business. If a manager initiates a project or subproject, he might obligate others to report back to him.

A Word of Caution

It would be easy to conclude that, because few managers devote the requisite time to planning, that the same approach is appropriate for project managers. Every major study that I have seen on the correlation between the project manager's actions and project success have shown planning to be vital.

> **Survival Tip: Just because very few managers spend much time on planning does not mean that project managers should abandon planning. If you have no plan, you have no control!**

It is a fact that project managers are supposed to be in control, in the sense of getting results from the project team. And since control is defined as comparing where you are to where you are supposed to be, so you can take corrective action when there is a deviation, it follows that if you have no plan you have no control, since you have nothing against which to compare your progress. For that reason, planning in not an option—it is a requirement! Perhaps if more general managers spent more time planning, we would have fewer organizations operating in crisis mode.

THINK LIKE A MANAGER

Because most project managers make a transition from doing some "technical" job to managing, many of them continue to think in terms of technical work rather than true management. The thinking of managers is laden with considerations of finance, strategy, and overall organizational issues. Money in particular occupies much of their thought. Not so with technologists, whether they be engineers, programmers, or scientists.

Think money!

You can't take forever and spend unlimited amounts of money.

Think Money

When I was an engineering manager, I had great difficulty getting my design engineers to understand that you couldn't take forever and spend unlimited amounts of money designing a product so it was *perfect*, which is what many of them wanted to do. It has always seemed strange to me that employees think organizations have an unlimited pot of gold, while they recognize that this is not true for themselves. True, there is a great deal of waste in organizations—even considerable extravagance. Staff sees senior management spending money on meetings in exotic locations when the meeting could have been held locally, and they get the feeling that money is no object. But this is not true.

In a company I was working with, a scientist had a brilliant idea for a new product. One of the marketing managers asked him what it would take to produce it. This product, said the scientist, would require about eight hours of time for a scientist to prepare in the lab—it couldn't really be done in production.

"Then you will have to sell it to a research lab for about $500," said the marketing person.

"Oh, a lab will never pay that much for it," said the scientist.

"Then you don't have a product," replied the marketer.

This is not, unfortunately, an isolated instance. This scientist had no idea, apparently, that you can't sell a product at or below the cost to produce it and stay in business for very long. Furthermore, he probably would have estimated the cost to be whatever he was paid per hour, multiplied by eight hours. But that is not the true cost: heat, water, lights, rent, lab equipment, insurance benefits, social security, unemployment insurance, and all the other things that the financial people call overhead (or burden, which is the term I like best), must also be reckoned with. The *loaded labor rate,* which is the person's salary plus the overhead, is usually 1.3 times the base pay of the person. So the real cost to produce would be anywhere from $50 to $75 an hour. For eight hours of work on this person's part, you will have spent $400, minimum, to produce the product. Even selling it at $500 does not yield a high enough margin. The general rule is that you must sell at twice the cost to produce in order to achieve an adequate profit that will keep you in business.

Your first concern as a manager is the economics of your activities. You must constantly be mindful of what it costs to do something, and the value of the benefit to be gained by doing it. In quality control, one of the basic principles of improving a process is to eliminate any step that adds no value to the product being produced. We should all think about that. If an activity adds no value to the organization, it should be eliminated.

Be Proactive, Not Reactive

As a technologist, you were often told what to do. As a manager, you don't wait to be told what to do. Rather, you look around and decide what must be done based on a clear understanding of what your project (or department) is supposed to accomplish. (Since this book is written for project managers, we will not concern ourselves with departmental issues.) If a project has a clear mission (which it should), then everything you do as a manager should contribute to the achievement of that mission.

As an example of how *not* to manage, I will relate an incident that happened several years ago. Two men from a university told me that they were responsible for refurbishing buildings on the campus, and they wanted to know what to do when a project was stalled. I asked for an example. One of them said, "Okay, you come in one day and realize that the natural

> **Survival Tip:** Take the initiative rather than wait to be told what to do.

gas has to be turned off in the building before some other work can be done, and you don't know how to go about getting this done. What do you do about things like that?"

I actually had a hard time believing he was serious. As a project manager, shouldn't this be part of the plan? Wouldn't you know that the gas would have to be turned off ahead of time? And wouldn't you make arrangements to have it done?

Well, maybe he was caught off guard by that one. Maybe it really didn't occur to him that the gas had to be turned off. So I asked for another example, and it was the same thing all over again: "You want to paint a room and it contains a big collating copier that must be moved by a copier technician. And you don't know who to contact." This is not project management—it isn't even very good project coordination! It is very reactive.

However, it does illustrate another probable cause of the problem. My guess is that these two were planning their projects unilaterally, without involving the group in the process. Surely, someone would have thought of these things had a group been involved!

Take Responsibility and Assume Authority

Related to the need to be proactive is the need for a manager to take responsibility for getting things done and to assume authority for it. I learned early in my career that I had as much authority as I was willing to assume. If you wait for someone to give it to you, it may never happen, because those who have the power to give you authority are looking for signs that you can deal with it; they don't see those signs so long as you operate in the passive, reactive mode.

I once had a friend, several years older than myself, who was fond of saying, "It's always easier to get forgiveness than permission." I have learned over the years that he was right. Of course, this doesn't mean that you do things that violate established policies about such things as spending limits, legal requirements, and so on. If your position in the organization entitles you to spend up to $1,000 of company money without prior approval, you don't spend $2,000 and then ask forgiveness. That will get you in trouble. But there are often areas in which you *think* you should ask your boss what to do, when really you should simply make that decision, and drive on. Senior managers have often told me that they wish their people would make their own decisions and take that burden away from them. They have more important things to deal with!

> **Survival Tip: Take responsibility for your actions, and assume that you have authority. The worst that can happen is that you may get your hands smacked.**

Understand Political Reality

Like it or not, every act in an organization has a political implication. Many technologists complain about politics. They wish they would go away, but they won't. The only realistic thing to do is to deal with organizational politics as best you can. I don't encourage anyone to play backstabbing politics, but you *do* need allies to further your causes. You can benefit from having friends in high places—and you can be hurt badly by someone who becomes an enemy.

> **Survival Tip: Be aware of political reality, and behave in ways that are in line with that reality.**

I recently was working with a company in which a new, enterprise-wide software system was being installed. Initially the project started in manufacturing. But one of the senior managers pointed out that, if the manufacturing person ran the project, it

Every act in an organization has a political impact.

—

That's life!

would be seen as strictly a manufacturing project and no one else in the building would have any interest in it. He wanted a person from another department to co-lead this project, and he also insisted that representatives from other affected departments be assigned. That was a good example of political reality. Had the project not been structured this way, I daresay it would have run into serious problems later on.

3

Types of Projects and the Project Manager

*A*ren't all projects alike? Can't they all be managed in the same way? If not, what demands does this place on project managers? Can the same person be effective in managing any type of project, or will different skills be required?

WHAT IS A PROJECT?

Before going too far, let me address this question: just what is a project, anyway? The Project Management Institute (PMI) makes the point in their Project Management Body of Knowledge (PMBOK®) document that one of the distinguishing features of a

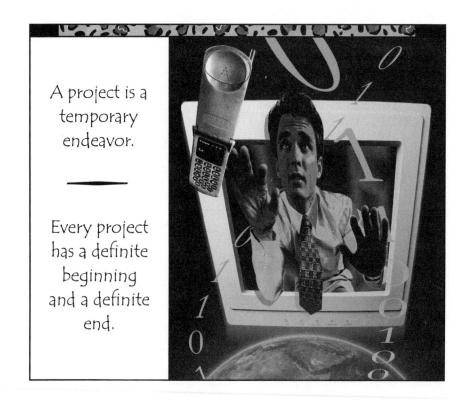

A project is a temporary endeavor.

―――

Every project has a definite beginning and a definite end.

project is that it is a *temporary* activity as opposed to a repetitive one. The repetitive activities performed in an organization are called *operations*, and usually fall under various functions (or departments), such as accounting or manufacturing. Projects may cut across functional "boundaries," actually involving personnel from many departments. An example of this would be the installation of an enterprise software system that affects every department. Such projects may be managed by an individual from the IS department, or by someone from the Project Office (if the organization has one).

PMI defines a project as follows:

> A project is a temporary endeavor undertaken to create a unique product or service. Temporary *means that every project has a definite beginning and a definite end.* Unique *means that the product or service is different in some distinguishing way from all other products or services (PMBOK 2000, p. 4; emphasis in original).*

42

Temporary

This word can be a bit confusing. Some projects take years to complete—designing an airliner; constructing a large dam, the pyramids, cathedrals in medieval times; and so on. So *temporary* is not synonymous with *short!*

Unique

This word also must be considered. Construction jobs would seem to be excluded from the definition of projects, because the same floorplan can be built in many different locations. True; but the terrain is different each time, the construction crew may be unique in every case, and the weather will vary, affecting work schedules. Thus, even what appears to be repetitive work can actually be unique when all factors are considered.

Types of Projects

For many years, I have defined "project" differently than the PMBOK. My definition has been:

> *A project is a multi-task, one-time job that has a definite starting point, definite ending point, well-defined scope of work, a budget, and temporary team.*

In my seminars, I have joked that you seldom find a project that conforms to this definition, but that we would like for them to, as it would make our lives easier. Even though this is so, discussions with my colleague and friend, Doug DeCarlo, have made me realize that some projects can't be made to conform to this definition. There are actually four types of projects. The category into which the job falls depends on two factors, which will be discussed in a moment.

It has been suggested that there are projects in which the goal is not known. I submit that this reflects a state of confusion between ends and means. The end is the desired outcome or result. The means used to achieve that end may not always be known, but one should *always* be able to define the end to be achieved.

For example, someone defines the end to be achieved as finding a cure for cancer. This is not a good definition the end to be achieved. It may be possible to prevent cancer (perhaps by way of a vaccination, though it also may be possible through gene therapy, assuming the cancer is genetically caused, not virally induced). A better definition would be that we want to eliminate suffering and death caused by cancer. This allows us to seek a cure, in the case that a person succumbs to the disease, or to work on a prevention method.

Developing a cure and developing a prevention method are both aimed at the *overall* goal—to eliminate suffering and death caused by cancer—but they employ different approaches or means.

Now, even when the desired end or result is known, we still don't know how to achieve it. We still don't have a vaccine or gene-based method of preventing cancer; we have only marginal cures so far; and research has been focused on both of these for about a century. This may be, in part, because we are unsure whether the *cause* of cancer is a virus or genetic (or some combination of the two). It may also be that there are many cancerlike diseases, with many different causes, so that each must be treated differently.

In any case, I can think of absolutely no project in which it is not possible to clearly state the desired end result, so I do not believe that *extreme* projects are those having no clear mission or goal. However, it certainly is possible to have extreme projects in the sense that we don't have a clue *how* to achieve the desired result (such as the cancer example).

Types of Problems

All projects are conducted to solve a problem of some kind. Problems fall into two categories, open- and closed-ended. A closed-ended problem has a *cause*, and therefore a solution. Either remove the cause or render it ineffective, and the problem is solved. Examples include repairing a car, curing a disease, solving a math problem, and so on. In some cases, the solution is to remove the cause, such as in repairing a car. If a component has become defective, you replace that part and the car should run properly. In curing a disease, the cause may be genetic. There are two possible solutions presently under study. One is to silence the gene that causes the disease. The other is gene splicing, in which the defective gene is replaced with a "healthy" one.

Open-ended problems do not have causes, nor do they have single solutions. Many open-ended problems can be thought of as results or outcomes we would like to bring about. We would like to penetrate a new market, develop a new product, colonize the moon, and so on. These are all problems to be solved, but there may be several approaches that will result in the desired outcome.

In the case of colonizing the moon, there is no ready solution. There are a number of possibilities. One is to build a space station, send astronauts to the station, then switch to another vehicle and proceed from there. Another is to build a very large, multi-stage rocket and propel voyagers to the moon through brute force. (This is an example of an ill-defined or unknown solution situation.)

Penetrating a new market is a problem for which some reasonably well-defined solutions exist. New markets have been penetrated in the past, and several approaches have been used. The solution is not highly defined, but at least it is not unknown.

Considering these two dimensions—open- and closed-ended problems, and well-defined or poorly defined solutions—we can define four kinds of projects, as shown in Table 3.1.

Poorly defined	Type II	Type IV
Well-defined	Type I	Type III
	Closed-ended	Open-ended

Table 3.1
Types of Projects

In Table 3.2, we see that the level of risk for each type of project also varies. This table provides some examples of each type of project.

Type of Project	Risk Level	Examples
Type I	Low	Construction, repair a car
Type II	Moderate-high	Cure a disease, crime prevention
Type III	Moderate-high	Simple IT project, product development
Type IV	Very high	Go to the moon, complex IT project

Table 3.2
Project Risk Levels

The Type I Project

The Type I project is a well-defined job. Typical of Type 1 is the construction project using conventional methods of building. These projects can be planned and scheduled with a fairly high degree of certainty about costs and time frame. An example is the competition that was held in 1983 by the Building Industry Association of San Diego to see how quickly a house could be built. This house was a conventional, single-family home, ranch-style, single-story, set upon a cement slab. Through elaborate planning, practice, and a refinement of methods, two houses were built simultaneously, and the winning team completed their house in 2 hours and 45 minutes! This included pouring the cement slab, landscaping the lawn, and installing typical amenities (such as an oven and carpeting). In other words, the house was ready to move into when it was finished.

It is important to note that this was not a prefabricated home. The teams began with raw lumber, wallboard, and so on. Furthermore, their supply of raw materials was not unlimited. If they damaged a piece of wallboard and ran out, the competition ended.

Of course, I know you have many questions. How do you pour concrete and cure it so fast? The teams put exothermic chemicals into the cement to cause it to set in 30 minutes. The joke was that it cured so fast, they had to be careful not to permanently cement a worker into the foundation. You are probably concerned about quality, too. It can't have been very good. Not so: San Diego building inspectors (wearing referee shirts) were on site to ensure that the work met standard building codes—which, in San Diego, are more stringent than in some other areas because of the earthquake threat.

46

There were 350 workers on each site, and many activities that would normally be done in sequence were performed simultaneously. For example, while the cement foundation was being poured, a group was nailing together the struts that would form the walls, and another was building the roof. When the slab was cured, the walls were carried over and placed in position; then the roof was hoisted by a crane and lowered into position. One team, in fact, got their roof on slightly crooked and had to detach it and reposition it. This probably cost them the competition.

This job was scheduled down to 10-minute increments. Furthermore, the previous week, the exact same house had been built, for practice, and required 6 hours to complete. The team then conducted a lessons-learned review, refined their plan, and reduced their time to half the previous value. (This illustrates the value of lessons-learned reviews.)

It is interesting to note that, even in this case of well-defined work, the plan predicted that the house would require 3 hours and 39 minutes to complete. The team therefore referred to it as the "4-hour house project." The fact that it required only 2 hours and 45 minutes illustrates what I said earlier in Chapter 1—all processes vary, and we must accept that variability. There is no such thing as a *deterministic* estimate!

The Type II Project

Finding a way to eliminate deaths caused by cancer is an example of a Type II project. We know what we want to do, but we have no clue (initially) how to do it. It is poorly defined, because, first of all, what causes cancer? Unless you know that, you won't be able to either cure or prevent it.

Sometimes fortuitous events occur. It was announced recently that a doctor has discovered that an anti-seizure drug greatly reduces hot flashes experienced by post-menopausal women. This was an accidental discovery. Now the researchers will work backward, from the "cure" to the cause of hot flashes, in order to understand why this drug works at all. This is not, of course, the common approach to finding a cure for a disease or malady.

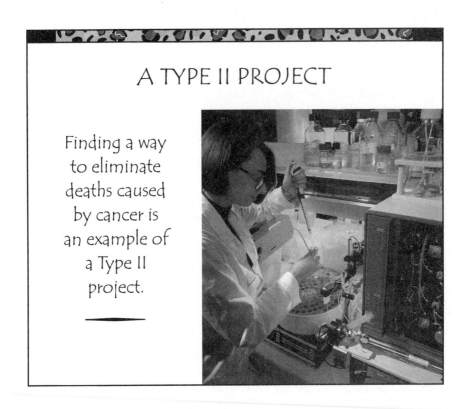

A TYPE II PROJECT

Finding a way to eliminate deaths caused by cancer is an example of a Type II project.

The thing is, even when you know the cause of a disease, you don't necessarily know how to cure or prevent it. Vaccinations for virally caused diseases have been very difficult to develop. I don't know all of the reasons for this, but one is that many viruses mutate so frequently that, just as a vaccine for one strain appears, another strain develops. Both the AIDS and influenza viruses do this.

If the cause of a disease is genetic, can you develop a cure? There are a number of avenues of investigation in this case. For example, can you splice a "healthy" gene into the spot where a "defective" gene exists, thus eliminating the cause of the disease? Or can you use silencing RNA (called siRNA) to suppress the offending gene? (Without going into detail, certain kinds of RNA will actually keep a gene from *expressing*. It turns out that, even though a gene may be present, it may not be active (or expressed); therefore, it causes no problem. In fact, it may be that in some cases a virus causes a nonexpressed gene to become active, thus causing a disease.)

The point is that such projects cannot be planned in great detail. However, I have had scientists take the extreme position that you cannot plan a research project. I tell them this is not true. You cannot plan in great detail, nor can you plan to the ultimate conclusion, but you surely can plan in phases. These projects have conditional branches. You do your experiments, studies, and so on, and you see what happens. Did it work? If *yes*, then you take a next step, called step 1. If *no*, then you take next step 2. This means that I can plan up to the conditional branch, just not with a great deal of precision. I don't know exactly how long some activities take, so my time-lines will be very broad-brushed, not very detailed. But I certainly should have some idea of what all I will do to answer the questions that must be answered in order to get me to that conditional branch.

Almost all pharmaceutical, biotech, and other kinds of research-driven projects fall into the Type II category, the extreme project category. These projects cannot be justified by ROI (return-on-investment) or NPV (net present value) analysis. I read once that in drug research, as many as 10,000 compounds may be examined before one is found that becomes a drug. By that time, as much as $50 to $100 million may have been spent on research. This is why drug companies must charge high prices. They must recover that investment before another company finds a compound that works as well, or better.

The Type III Project

The Type III project is open-ended, which means it has no single solution. However, it is fairly well defined. Some simple IT and product development projects fall into this category. We know exactly what we want to do, but there are a number of ways to get there. These projects generally have moderate to high risk. One reason is that, even though we begin with well-defined requirements, those requirements tend to change over time. This is especially true for projects that last for a year or more. There is almost sure to be a change in the environment that will require us to adapt to it. A competitor will bring out a product that has features we did not plan to incorporate into our product. Users realize they

For projects that last over a year, there is almost sure to be a change in the environment that requires us to adapt.

have forgotten some feature, or they realize that a feature is possible that no one thought of originally.

For this reason, some people advocate breaking long projects into three- to six-month phases, so that fewer changes are likely to be required during each phase. Also, one of the plagues of all long-term projects is that resources are yanked to put out fires in other areas of the organization. This is less likely to happen if the project phase is of short duration.

Type IV Projects

If any type of project can be called extreme, this category probably fits the bill. The problem is open-ended, so multiple solutions are possible. It is very poorly defined. We know we want *something*—we just aren't sure exactly what it is, nor do we know how to produce it. This may be exemplified by developing a very complex IT program—for instance, the graphical user interface (GUI).

For those of you too young to remember DOS, early personal computers required that operating instructions be entered manually. At best, you had a software program with menus from which you could select, but you still had to enter many commands manually. It was tedious and kept a lot of people from using personal computers, because they either couldn't or didn't want to learn all those commands. So a lot of software developers were searching for a better way.

At that point, this was an open-ended problem that was also poorly defined. How could you operate the computer without entering instructions manually? How could you make it possible for computer-illiterate individuals to become proficient users of computers? Do you change the people or the computer to solve the problem?

Xerox developed the solution. Its Altos system—copied by Apple—used icons on the screen to launch programs, execute complex command instructions, and so on. This approach made *personal* computers accessible to many more individuals than would ever have been possible using the old DOS system. Interestingly, Xerox was uncertain whether the computer would be accepted in the marketplace, so they waffled long enough that Apple released the Macintosh. The rest is history.

Now, when you set out to design a GUI system, there are many different ways to do it. The Apple and Windows systems may be very similar, in that both are graphical user interfaces, but there are also many differences. If you go back to when these systems were first being designed, I bet you'd find multiple changes to the implementation as the projects progressed (that is, the scope changed greatly).

Projects like this, in short, cannot be planned with the same degree of certainty as a construction project. Estimates of task durations are not nearly as good in a Type IV project as in a Type I, because for Type I projects you generally have a history on which to base your estimates. You've done many of these tasks before and you know *about* how long they take. In writing software, or developing rockets, however, you don't have so much history (at least at the time the space program started, this was true), so you can expect your estimates to be much less certain than in construction. Therefore, the risk of not meeting targets is higher than for the Type I project. For a Type I project, you can sometimes schedule work to 10-minute increments (as was done in the 4-hour house project). For Type II, III, and IV projects, you may not be able to do better than the nearest week—or even month, for that matter!

SKILLS REQUIRED

As you might expect, the skills required to manage projects depend on the type of project. The Type I project is well defined, low risk, with a well-known solution. The Type IV project is extreme in being neither well defined or having clear-cut solutions. A project manager for a Type IV project will most likely need a high level of conceptual thinking ability, because if you can't conceptualize the problem, you can't solve it. Even the Type I project can be of a magnitude that requires a high degree of conceptual skills, but it is still less demanding than the Type IV.

Another Source of Complexity

In our book, *World-Class Project Manager,* Bob Wysocki and I (2000) identified technical and organizational complexity as another source of difficulty. Technical complexity probably needs no explanation, but what is meant by "organizational complexity"?

A simple and traditional form of organization structure is the simple hierarchy, in which a person has a single supervisor, who in turn has a supervisor. Figure 3.1 shows such a structure.

If this were the structure of a project, it would be called a pure-project organization, and it would be relatively easy for a project manager to deal with. In this situation, you "own" your resources—no one can take them unless they ask. Every person has a single supervisor, so lines of authority and communication are clear. A novice project manager could probably handle small projects with this structure.

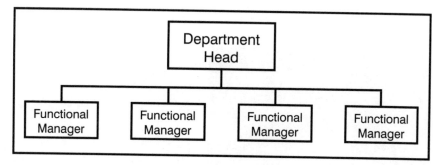

Figure 3.1
Hierarchical Organization

The matrix organization is another issue, however. In a matrix, the organization itself may be hierarchical and functionally organized, but project managers must "borrow" their resources from those functional groups, which creates a structure as shown in Figure 3.2. This kind of structure demands strong interpersonal skills, as well as more years of experience, to manage effectively.

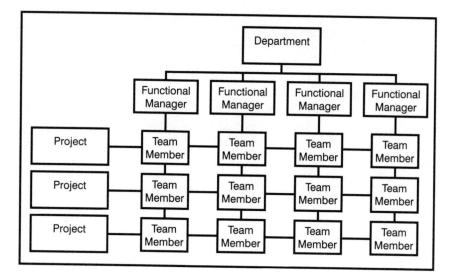

Figure 3.2
Matrix Organization Structure

Assessing
Yourself

Good interpersonal
skills and experience
are key to managing
effectively.

Assessing Yourself

If you would like to assess yourself to see how you "stack up" in terms of these kinds of requirements, Bob Wysocki has developed online assessments and has them available on his web site: www.eiiinc.com. Note also his organizational readiness assessment, which is used to determine if an organization is ready for project management.

4

Dealing Effectively with People

A person who wants to be an engineer spends at least four years in a university studying the principles of engineering. The same is true of programming, medicine, and other professions. Yet, organizations make managers of people who have no formal education in how to deal with the core component of their job—people!

As Dr. Phil McGraw has said, "No matter how smart you are, if you haven't got the training, we cannot strap you into the cockpit of a 747, launch you off the end of the runway, and expect you to know how to fly that airplane. The problem is that when it comes to succeeding at the game of life, nobody ever really taught you the rules, let alone how to play the game" (1999, p. 40).

One thing I learned in my doctoral program in psychology is that people behave consistently with their deeply held beliefs about the world. This being the case, you can tell what

Will people skills become virtually nonexistent ?

people really believe by watching their behavior. Apparently, many managers believe that you need no training in how to deal with people. You are no doubt born with that ability. And many do not value this skill because they themselves lack it. Sorry, but that's the fact of the matter. They believe that if you know how to handle the technical aspects of the job, you can manage effectively.

As Dr. Phil says, "Since we do not get formal training from society [in how to deal with each other], we've been relying on the role models in our lives . . . [but] if our parents were never *trained* to be effective mothers, fathers, spouses, then what kind of role models could they be?" (1999, p. 41). The same could be said for using other managers as role models. How many of them actually know how to deal effectively with people?

Please understand that I intend to demean no one. We are all a product of our background, and for the past century, teaching "people" skills has not been part of American culture. What little has been taught has tended to be—to use Stephen Covey's (1989) expression—"personality ethic," which means how to manipulate people to get what you want, even if it is to their disadvantage. Maybe that is why Dale Carnegie's book, *How to Win Friends and Influence People,* has continued to be a best-seller for nearly 50 years. It is more substantive and fills a need not being met in other ways.

Even psychology courses tend to be unhelpful, because they too often focus on the biological causes of behavior and on theory; they provide little guidance on how to actually deal with other people in positive, productive ways. And now that a generation of young people is coming along who have spent the better part of their lives glued to a computer screen, people skills may well become virtually nonexistent.

UNDERSTANDING BEHAVIOR

Some fundamental principles guide my thinking about why people behave as they do:

1. People hold beliefs about what the world is like, which are called *models of reality.*

2. People form and preserve their models through three perceptual processes. These are called *deletion, distortion,* and *generalization.* Deletion is the failure to notice evidence that would challenge the person's beliefs. Distortion is the failure to interpret evidence in such a way that the belief would be challenged. Generalization is the process in which a single instance of something happening is taken as evidence that the entire world is like the single example.

3. People always behave consistently with their models of the world—that is, what they believe to be true about the world around them. These beliefs are about people, nature, economics, and so on.

4. In order for a person to change his or her behavior, the model governing that behavior must be changed (that

The individual is not his or her behavior.

Don't characterize a person entirely by behavior.

Bad Mad or Crazy?

is, the person's belief about that facet of the world must change).

5. All behavior is an attempt to satisfy the needs of the individual.

6. Because the individual may have learned only one behavior that has worked in the past, he or she can be said to be making the best or only choice available for satisfying the given need.

7. The individual is *not* his or her behavior! We tend to label people "bad, mad, or crazy" because of the negative impact of their behavior, but the person is no more his or her behavior than a computer is its programs.

8. All behavior makes sense from the perspective of the actor. The only reason it seems inexplicable to us is that we do not share that person's perspective.

Let's examine these points one by one.

Points 1 & 2

The first point states that people hold beliefs about reality—*their* model of the world, or to use a popular term, a *paradigm*. As I mentioned above, these beliefs are about everything that concerns us—people, businesses, nature, the world itself, religion, economics, and so on. Our parents, teachers, or friends may pass these beliefs to us, or they may be formed based on our experience in the world. For example, our friends often pass prejudices to us. If we have a racist friend, we may believe that people of other races are bad. If we have never had direct experience interacting with someone from another race, we have no way of knowing if they actually are bad, but if we trust our friends we may accept their belief as fact.

Interestingly, even if we do interact with someone of another race, if the belief is very strong, then we may not notice that the person is actually not so bad after all. This is the process we called *deletion* above (see Point 2). We actually do not notice evidence that would challenge the belief.

But what if some other friend were to say, "That person is not actually so bad." Then you may get *distortion*. You reply, "He was just on his good behavior around us. But I believe people of that race are bad."

Through the processes of deletion and distortion, an incorrect belief can be maintained indefinitely. Another way to say this is that a belief functions as a filter—causing us to see only evidence that would con-

> *There is no reality—only perception.*

firm what the belief tells us is true, and overlooking evidence that would disconfirm it.

Particle physicists have learned in the past century that the very act of observing atomic particles causes the interactions to be changed, and they have concluded that we can never be certain about what is actually real—all we have is perception. In terms of how we behave, however, it can be restated that perception *is* reality to us, because we will behave as if what we perceive is absolutely true, regardless of the *objective* facts of the situation!

Point 3

The third point is very important for understanding people. They always behave consistently with their beliefs. It doesn't matter what they *say* they believe, you can tell what they really believe by observing their behavior. The reason for this is that people do not always know what they really believe. Because it is socially unacceptable to be racially prejudiced, a person may claim to be unbiased. Observation, however, may prove him to be biased. Chris Argyris (1990) has called this one's *theory espoused* versus *theory-in-use.*

As I noted earlier, we can tell that many managers do not believe you need any training in how to deal with people, because they won't invest in it. A few years ago, when project management training was in very high demand, I did 40 three-day seminars in one year. During that same year, I only did three or four seminars on people skills. Companies simply don't see the need.

Point 4

If a person's behavior is to change, his or her belief governing that behavior must change. The problem is that changing a person's belief can be extremely difficult, as I have already said. We tend to preserve our beliefs through deletion and distortion. We also tend to go into denial when someone challenges them.

For example, consider a person who has developed a problem with alcohol. When confronted, she claims that she has no problem—that she is a social drinker only, and can quit any time she wants. Alcoholics Anonymous has always maintained that they cannot help an alcoholic until that person admits to having a drinking problem. It seems these individuals must sometimes hit "rock bottom" before they admit their problem. Usually this means that their spouses have abandoned them, they have lost their job, or worse, may have killed someone in a drunk-driving accident.

Point 5

All behavior is an attempt to satisfy the needs of the individual. That's right—*all!* Even criminal behavior. Not all of those needs have positive implications, but they are needs nevertheless. For example, a criminal may be trying to prove that he is a better man than anyone else, so he bullies people, develops sadistic tendencies, and perhaps even resorts to murder—all in an attempt to satisfy his need for power or the need to feed his ego.

Point 6

In the case of the criminal mentioned in the previous paragraph, this individual may have learned to feed his ego only by bullying people. He never learned that he could feel good about himself by doing positive, achievement-oriented things. It may be that nothing he ever did was good enough for his parents, so achievement gave him no satisfaction. Whatever the case, most people are making the best or only choices available to them in behaving as they do.

Point 7

The individual is not his or her behavior, but we don't tend to see it that way. In fact, we tend to characterize the person *entirely* by his or her behavior. Children who behave badly are called "bad" children. Unfortunately, such labeling has been found to convey to children how they are *expected* to be—if we are going to call them bad, then that must be what we expect of them, so they try to comply. One reason, as Dr. Phil points out in his book, is that the number one fear people (and children) have is the fear of rejection; and conversely, the number one need is to be accepted. People will do whatever it takes to be accepted by those who are important to them.

Point 8

All behavior makes sense from the perspective of the actor. An individual's behavior may not make sense to us, but that is only because we don't share that person's perspective. I recently had that brought home to me while consulting to a company. They were talking about changing an enterprise software system. I thought they should take a good look at all available products rather than just upgrade their existing system, as I had heard numerous negatives about it. When I mentioned this to the company president, he said that they did not want to spend a huge amount of money on a new system because they were getting ready to launch a public stock offering and wanted the bottom line to look as healthy as possible. From his perspective, upgrading the existing product was the *only* thing that made sense.

In fact, in my nearly 40 years of working experience, I have learned that the clashes that exist between senior managers and lower-level employees is often this difference in perspective, and senior managers are not at liberty to tell employees what goes on behind the scenes. For that reason, Dr. Covey (1989) has a very important principle for us: "Seek first to understand, then to be understood."

DR. PHIL'S CHARACTERISTICS OF PEOPLE

The principles I have outlined are my own guidelines to understanding people. Dr. Phil lists ten others in his book, *Life Strategies*, that I think are worth remembering. In fact, he says in his book that if you need to, write these on the back of your hand so you will remember them. I agree with him.

1. The number one fear among all people is rejection.
2. The number one need among all people is acceptance.
3. To manage people effectively, you must do it in a way that protects or enhances their self-esteem.
4. Everybody—and I mean everybody—approaches every situation with at least some concern about "what's in it for me?"
5. Everybody—and I mean everybody—prefers to talk about things that are important to them personally.
6. People hear and incorporate only what they understand.
7. People like, trust, and believe those who like them.

8. People often do things for other than the apparent reasons.

9. Even people of quality can be, and often are, petty and small.

10. Everybody—and I mean everybody—wears a social mask. You must look beyond the mask to see the person.

APPLYING THESE CHARACTERISTICS IN PROJECTS

If you merely read this list and say, "Oh, yes, that sounds reasonable," you will have completely missed their importance. The knowledge must be applied—not just occasionally, but daily! And, with everyone with whom you interact—team members, customers, suppliers, your boss, your co-workers. If you do so, you will gain an edge on those who remain clueless about these principles.

> *The difference between winners and losers is that winners do things losers don't want to do.*
> — **Dr. Phillip McGraw**

Let's examine them one by one and see how they can be applied in your projects.

The Number One Fear

The number one fear is rejection. This leads to fear of failure, since failing may cause others to reject you. It may mean fear of taking risks, since taking risks may lead to failure and rejection. And failing to take risks means you are stifling innovation and creativity, both of which involve taking risks.

There is no telling how much of an impact this fear has in the workplace, but my guess is that it is enormous. People will tell you what they think you want to hear, rather than risk being rejected because they told you the facts. In my programs on teams, I teach people how to give and receive feedback effectively. This is especially

The impact of fear in the workplace is probably considerable.

important when it comes to managing conflict in your team. Yet I find it is one of the big barriers to improving performance. The marginal performer is left alone. Rather than confront the person's performance deficit, it is ignored. The reason? The manager is afraid of the emotional reaction that will undoubtedly result. We all know that when we give people "constructive feedback," they get defensive and lash out at us. The reason is that they feel rejected, and thereby hurt, and they respond by trying to hurt back.

No problem can be solved unless it is acknowledged and confronted, and avoiding the emotional outburst just leads to an eventual disaster. In many organizations, marginal employees have been in their jobs for years and yet their supervisors give them satisfactory performance evaluations. The supervisors are afraid to "tell it like it is" and risk the wrath of the employee. For one thing, this would mean that the employee rejects the supervisor, so this is an insidious vicious circle.

As project manager, you must try very hard not to make anyone feel rejected. This means you must not practice exclusionary tactics that leave you with an inner circle and the rest of the tribe excluded. You must share information, because withholding information is a signal that you reject people. If you invite certain people to meetings and omit others, you send a rejection signal to those excluded. (Since you can't include everyone, you must let the excluded people know that they are not being rejected.

> **Survival Tip:** Be very careful not to make people feel rejected by you.

One way to do this is to ensure that there are occasional meetings where you update *everyone* on the project.)

Another simple practice that pays dividends: Answer *all* e-mail! Yes, I know some of the e-mail you receive is just for-your-information (fyi) and some is sent by people trying to protect themselves. But your answer need consist of only one sentence: "Thanks for keeping me informed." It takes a few seconds to write that reply, which acknowledges the person who has taken the time to notify you.

When you don't answer e-mail, you reject the sender. I correspond with many people, and I have observed that the really effective managers always answer my e-mail. It may be a one-word response, but it is a response. I try to keep my communications with Alan Mulally brief, because I know he is extremely busy, but he *always* responds. Other people I deal with, who are not nearly as busy as Alan, don't answer. Whether they mean to or not, they say to me that I am not important enough for them to take the time to answer. (If any of you are reading this—and you know who you are—answer my darned e-mails! *Hi!*)

> **EXERCISE:** *Reflect on the ways in which you may be inadvertently sending rejection signals to people. Write them down. One way to approach this is to think of things people do that make you feel "put down" and rejected. Once you have your list, think of ways to behave differently to avoid doing this.*

Number One Need

The number one need of people is acceptance. This is, of course, the reverse side of the first characteristic—fear of rejection. They go hand-in-hand. You must make the people you deal with feel that you accept them, warts and all. It is easy to reject people because they have faults. Conversely, it also can be difficult to *accept*

> **Survival Tip:** **Treat people in ways that make them feel accepted.**

people who have certain kinds of flaws. Nevertheless, the first rule of dealing with people is that *you must deal with them where they are, not where you want them to be.* Until you do that, you can't help them overcome their flaws. If you remember that *people are not their behavior*, the going will be easier.

> **Survival Tip:** **Deal with people where they are, not where you want them to be.**

This doesn't mean that you condone unacceptable behavior. But separate the behavior from the person! I can care about you as a person, although I don't accept your problem behavior. Unfortunately, people tend to think that if you reject their behavior you reject them as a person, and in many cases that is exactly what we do because we equate the two.

There will be people who won't let you practice this principle. There are those who go through life with a chip on their shoul-

> **Survival Tip:** **Separate the behavior from the person. Remember, you are not your behavior!**

ders, asking you to knock it off. They are begging to be rejected. Some have felt rejected for so long that they cannot believe anyone could accept them; thus, their belief becomes a self-fulfilling proph-

ecy. And there is nothing you could do to convince them that you really accept them. Remember: Beliefs act as filters.

Enhance Self-Esteem

This is very similar to the need for acceptance. People need to feel good about themselves. For many of us, that feeling comes from knowing that others feel good about us. When you constantly criticize a person, the effect is to destroy that person's self-esteem.

There is a caution here. For many years, the schools have tried to build children's self-esteem, to make them feel good about themselves. The belief is that if they have high self-esteem, they will perform better. However, as Charles Sykes (1995) has written, there are no studies that have demonstrated that high self-esteem leads to good performance. There are many studies that show that high performance leads to high self-esteem. We have put the cart before the horse.

> **Survival Tip:** Deal with people so that you make them feel good about themselves.

We need to stroke people for good performance, not good intentions. Phony stroking of people in the belief that this will make them perform better simply doesn't work. In fact, it tends to have the opposite effect. The person may reason (at the unconscious level perhaps) that if you stroke him for marginal performance, then you really don't expect very much, and so he doesn't perform very well.

> **Survival Tip:** Reward people for good results, not good intentions.

The most respectful thing you can do for another human being is expect him to perform at the very highest level of which he is capable. To expect less is to show disrespect for the person. You are saying, in effect, "You poor thing. We can't expect much of you. You're functionally incompetent."

For some of you, stroking people is difficult. You may find it easy to trash a person, but giving strokes is nearly impossible. You may have

> **Survival Tip:** Always demand from yourself and others the highest performance of which you and they are capable. Anything less is disrespectful.

been taught that there is no need to tell people they are doing well. Or you may simply feel uncomfortable expressing positive feelings.

Whatever the reason, you should remember this. One of the most important things for an employee is to know that the supervisor thinks highly of the his or her work. Again, this means that

> **Survival Tip: The most important opinion about an employee's performance is that of the supervisor (the project manager, in our case). Let people know when you feel they do good work!**

the supervisor accepts the person. This, in turn, boosts the individual's self-esteem. If you miss this point, you may as well hang up your supervisor's hat and go back to technical work. You'll never be very effective at the job. And I'm serious.

What's in It for Me?

I often call this the most important principle of dealing with people, but maybe I have ranked it too highly. It is the "What's in it for me?" (WIIFM) principle.

> **Survival Tip: You must be sure there is a payoff for a team member if he or she is to contribute to your team.**

People engage in what they do because there is a payoff. You may not like hearing this, but it is true. Yes, even benevolence falls into this category. The payoff is the warm feeling that you have done something good for others. If you didn't get that warm feeling, you wouldn't do the good deeds.

One of the first principles of getting people committed to a project team is to help them realize the benefits participation brings them. As a project manager, you must help meet the needs of the organization while simultaneously meeting the needs of every contributor. Remember Vance Packard's definition of leadership: Leadership is the art of getting others to want to do something you feel should be done. The key to getting them to want to do it is to demonstrate that their contributions will receive a fair exchange. If you can't do this, they will cease contributing.

Since the two highest human needs are acceptance and high self-esteem, do you see that the greatest reward is actually the intangible strokes—not that old demigod, money? Clearly, you can't give people strokes and withhold money, as they have survival needs as well as the need for self-esteem. But so long as the money is satisfactory, intangible needs will be the most important.

Money and intangible needs are critical to success.

So make sure everyone's needs are met.

What's in it for me?

Talk about Things Important to the Other Person

When we talk with others, we tend to discuss things that are important to us. That means it is pretty easy to tell what another person thinks is important—he or she will be talking about it. The thing is, if you just talk about what is important to you and don't respond to others about the things that

> **Survival Tip:** Talk about things that are important to the other person, not just those that are important to you.

are important to them, you will be seen as a boor.

I have some difficulty with this sometimes. I am not a sports enthusiast. I don't dislike sports, I just don't follow them. For some individuals, sports are synonymous with life itself. They live and breathe sports. Since I don't follow sports, or share their interest, it makes it hard for me to talk with them about their favorite subject.

Nevertheless, there is one topic that is always safe ground. People are always concerned about themselves, so if I get them talking about their interests, family, job, or whatever, then I can offset my limitation about sports. I must say that there is a major caution here. If you have no genuine interest in other people, faking it will backfire. Folks catch on

> **Survival Tip: People always like to talk about themselves. Show a genuine interest in the person, and you are halfway home!**

quickly. But I would also say to you that you shouldn't be a manager if you don't care about people.

As Gerald A. Michaelson (2001) has written:

> *Military writers also agree that an important quality of an ideal leader is a concern for people. In* On the Psychology of Military Incompetence, *Dixon points out that humanitarianism is a prerequisite for high morale and physical health (p. 19).*

People Hear What They Understand

The principle fully stated is that people hear and incorporate only what they understand. There is a big difference between information and meaning. If I tell a group that the stock market is down, it will mean something entirely different to the person who owns stock than to the person who does

> **Survival Tip: Be sure people understand your communication if you want them to act on it.**

not. They both receive the same information, but it has different meaning to each of them.

Often in projects, we convey information to people without ensuring that they understand it. Information that is not understood is meaningless to people, so they don't incorporate it into their daily work.

The difficulty is that people often hate to admit that they don't understand something you have told them. In fact, if you ask, "Do you understand?" they will nod their heads then go off and ask someone else to explain to them what you said. Worse yet, they will go off and act on what they *thought* you said, and that can be a disaster.

One way to ensure that the other person has understood you is to ask that he or she repeat what you've said in his or her own words. However, this may offend some individuals. It seems to imply that you believe they are dense. I always say, "Let me be sure I conveyed this to you clearly. Could you summarize for me what we are talking about, in your own words?" This signals that I may not have communicated very well, thus taking the other person off the hook.

You may also ask the other person to give you some idea how she will respond to what you have said. That is, what is she going to do about what you've just told her? If her response is totally out of line, it may be because she misunder-

> **Survival Tip:** Be sure others actually *do* understand what you have conveyed.

stood, and then you can work with her to ensure that she does understand. Remember, communication is a two-way street!

If You Like Me, I'll Probably Like You

It is characteristic that people like, trust, and believe those who like them. If you have ever dealt with a manager who is distant, perhaps even standoffish, you probably didn't know where you stood with that manager. You certainly didn't feel he liked you. The net result is that, while you may not have

> **Survival Tip:** Try to be a likeable person—and try to like most people.

disliked him, you definitely didn't like him either. You also may not have trusted him or believed what he told you.

Of course, you may have had the misfortune to have trusted and believed in someone you really liked only to learn that he or she was a snake in the grass. Perhaps you even have fallen into the trap of never trusting anyone again because you got burned that one time. This is an example of generalization, which I discussed

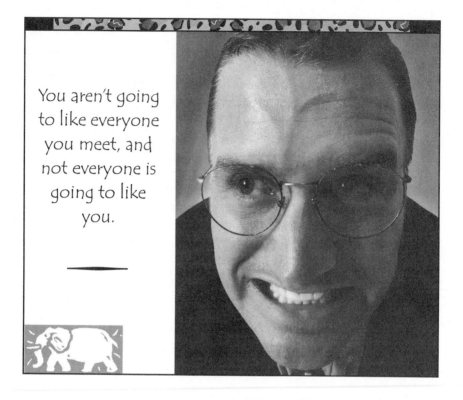

You aren't going to like everyone you meet, and not everyone is going to like you.

earlier in this chapter. One bad experience, and you are convinced everyone if just like this one snake.

Life is full of potholes. If you stay off the road because you're afraid of hitting a pothole, you won't go very far. And if you avoid people because one snake bit you, life is going to be pretty lonely.

You aren't going to like everyone you meet, and not everyone is going to like you. But on balance, isn't it better to *like* most people rather than to *dislike* most of them?

I remember the old saying, "There's a little good in the worst of us and a little bad in the best of us." If you can look for the good in everyone, it becomes easier to like them. And it is also helpful to remember: We're all more alike than we are different.

The Reason Isn't Apparent

This principle states that people often do things for other than the apparent reasons. We sometimes call this a *hidden agenda*. They propose things in meetings that seem to make no sense. That is because you are looking at the *apparent* reason for the suggestion without being aware of the person's hidden agenda. She pushes for engaging someone in Europe to help with the project. The reason—she wants to travel to Europe at company expense. Or a person volunteers for an assignment even though he isn't the best person for it. The

> **Survival Tip:** If a person's behavior makes no sense, look for the hidden agenda that may be behind it.

reason—he sees this as an opportunity to gain visibility to senior management, thus hoping to advance his career.

Remember the premise stated earlier, that behavior always makes sense to the actor. It may not make sense to you or me, but it does to him or her.

We Can All Be Petty and Small

Even people of quality can be, and often are, petty and small. For me, this means I need to cut everyone some slack sometimes. I think that when people behave in petty or small ways, it is usually because they are hurting for some reason. They have been injured, and they are "getting back" at the world for the injury. They

> **Survival Tip:** Cut people some slack when they behave in petty ways, so long as this is not the norm for them.

may lash out at you because you are convenient, or because they can't hit back at the person who actually inflicted the injury.

This is called *displaced aggression*. I have seen it in children, adults, and animals. A child will sometimes go beat up another child because one larger than herself has injured her, and she is afraid to fight back. So she beats a child smaller than herself. I have had many cats for pets, and sometimes if I roughhouse with one of them and get a little too rough, she will go jump on another cat, since she perceives that I am too big for her to whip. If the other cat could talk, it would probably say, "Why are you picking on me? I didn't do anything to you." I think we feel the same way when someone behaves in a petty way toward us and we did nothing to "deserve" it.

People Wear Masks

Everybody—and I mean everybody—wears a social mask. You must look beyond the mask to see the person. In fact, the word "personality" is derived from the word *persona,* which means *mask.* When I first started using the Myers-Briggs Type Indicator (MBTI) for personality assessment, people asked me why they felt that it didn't quite peg them. They felt it might be true in one setting but not in another. At first, I had no answer. Then I realized a very important truth: *We are different people in different places!*

At work, I may be a lean, mean, decision-making machine. At home, I may be a couch potato, indecisive as hell, and anything but lean and mean. One reason is that, after spending all day making decisions, I don't want to make any at home.

I also may be a highly social fellow at work and a recluse at home. Again, I've spent all day in social activities and now I need time to rejuvenate myself, to recharge my batteries. As I tell people when I teach a long seminar—no offense, but at the end of the day, I've become saturated and I don't want to go out and party with you. I want to go back to my hotel room, order room service, and vegetate.

It is important for us as managers to realize that some people try to present themselves as peacocks when they are really snakes. These are the dangerous ones. They can often be spotted because they are just a little too darned perfect. They have no warts at all. God makes A's on tests. They make B's, and

> **Survival Tip:** If they look too good to be true, they probably aren't.

everyone else makes C's, D's, or F's. Give me a break. Nobody's that perfect! But, even if they were, they probably wouldn't want to associate with me!

IN SUMMARY

One of Dr. Phil's suggestions is that you test these characteristics for yourself. Become a keen observer of people. I am confident that you will be able to validate the principles. When you see what appears to be an exception, ask yourself if you are missing something. You probably are.

> **EXERCISE:** *As an exercise, I suggest that you apply these principles and characteristics in your day-to-day project work. As an example, I learned during my career as a project manager that my relationships with functional managers—who owned the resources assigned to my project—were key to my success. I made it a point to get to know them, to be friendly with them, to learn about their concerns and try to always be considerate of them. Then, when I needed a favor from them, I was much more likely to get it from a functional manager with whom I had a good relationship than one whom I barely knew.*

One caution, however: As I have already said, you must genuinely care about people and their concerns. If you try to fake it, they will detect your insincerity, and your efforts at friendliness will backfire on you.

5

Managing Effectively

*I*n *Chapter 2,* we examined the role of the project manager. In particular, I said that you must be proactive—you must take the lead, set the pace and context, and provide your team a sense of direction. I especially believe that you must begin a project by conveying to your team a compelling vision for where the project is headed, what it is supposed to accomplish.

Vision is an image, whether actual or conceptual, that defines the final state of the project; that is, the final outcome. Unless you achieve a shared vision in your team, individuals will take you where *they* think you are going, rather than where you actually want to go. In addition, the vision must be compelling. It must be important, noteworthy, something your team can aspire to achieve. If it is ho-hum, they will have very little incentive to pursue it. Warren Bennis (2000) called it *managing the dream.*

Managers
- Take the lead
- Set the pace
- Provide a sense of direction

Instincts for Success

In case you are uncertain about the difference between vision and mission, it is easy to differentiate them. The mission of a project is always to achieve the vision. You begin with the vision. What do you want to achieve, produce, develop, or build? Of course, as Sun Tzu wrote in *The Art of War*, the vision must be developed with an awareness of reality (Michaelson, 2001, p. 3). For example, it may be possible to design a passenger plane that will fly at Mach 4, but as the Concorde has demonstrated, it is not likely to be an economically successful product.

> **Survival Tip:** Be sure that you have a shared vision in your team.

DON'T OVERLOOK STRATEGY

It is very important that you develop an effective project strategy before you develop an implementation plan. Strategy refers to the

Develop a project strategy **before** you develop an implementation plan.

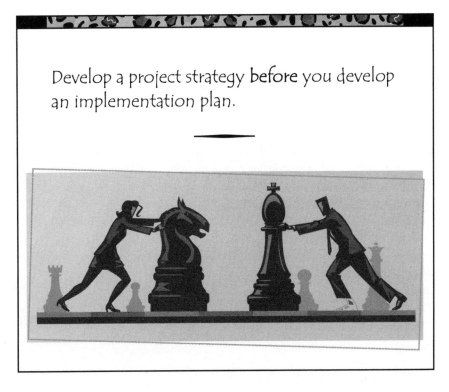

overall approach you will follow to do the job. All too often, teams fall back on what they have always done, without asking if there may be a better way. When Boeing developed the 777 airplane, they departed from conventional approaches in two significant ways. First, they adopted three-dimensional computer modeling, rather than doing two-dimensional paper drawings of each component of the plane. This allowed them to detect interfering parts inside a wing, for example, thereby making it possible to resolve the inter-

> **Survival Tip:** Choose a project strategy that is the *best* approach, not just the one you have always followed.

ference before any hardware was ever built. This must have reduced rework dramatically, and since nearly 30 percent of all project work is rework, on a $5 billion project, the savings could be enormous.

Second, the traditional approach to designing a product is to develop a part, throw the drawings over the wall to the next group that must do something with them, and so on. Boeing adopted a *Working Together* (Lewis, 2002) approach, in which participation and frequent communication were the norm. In addition, key suppliers were treated as members of the design team and kept completely in the loop. The same was true of the customer, pilots, and other major stakeholders. United Airlines had representatives on the team, so that the airplane would be designed to best meet the airlines' needs. Chief test pilot John Cashman, who flew the first 777, represented the interests of pilots, because this plane was a fly-by-wire model, rather than one that uses cables that actually physically move the wing and rudder controls (see Sabbagh, 1996, for a complete exposition on the development of the 777). Overall, this change in strategy allowed Boeing to produce a plane that is widely regarded as the most technologically advanced passenger plane flying today.

TACTICAL PLANNING

"The tactical implementation plan is as important as the strategic plan, because it takes the vision and strategy to the point of contact" (Michaelson, 2001, p. 11). It is here that a project manager can get into trouble, by going into planning paralysis. As Sun Tzu wrote:

> *The important thing is to get started. Too much time spent in planning can breed indecisiveness and error. It is often better to engage in some form of simultaneous planning and implementation.*

Michaelson says, "This can be as difficult as changing a tire while the car is moving. Tactical plans must be shaped in relation to reality with the information learned from contact" (op cit., p. 11).

> **Survival Tip: Time spent on implementation planning must be balanced: Neither too much nor too little.**

The key word is *balance.* Too much planning leads to paralysis; too little yields a "ready-fire-aim" approach that almost always leads to disaster. Type I projects lend themselves to very detailed planning. Type IV projects must be planned as you go.

A very important thing to remember about implementation plans is that circumstances may require them to be changed. Quoting Sun Tzu again:

> *In every endeavor, the abnormal is normal and uncertainty is certain. A contingency plan should be prepared to allow for the abnormal. The exercise of preparing the contingency plan yields insights into threats and opportunities (op cit., p. 12).*

This is commonly called risk management, and it is another frequently over-looked component of project planning.

> **Survival Tip:** Always expect the unexpected to happen!

COMMUNICATION PLANNING

I don't think I've ever talked with members of a project team who didn't tell me that they had communication problems. People don't get information at all, or they receive it in garbled form or too late in order for them to respond effectively. People refuse to talk with each other. Managers hoard information from their teams in order to maintain power over them. All of these maladies infect project teams and lead to a slow demise.

Communication skills are without a doubt among the most important skills a project manager must have. Without them, it is doubtful that a person will prove to be a good leader—people generally don't willingly follow someone who is unable to articulate what he

> **Survival Tip:** Communicate, communicate, communicate!

or she wants done. There is even a "big mouth" theory of leadership that asserts that individuals who express themselves well, and forcefully, are likely to emerge as leaders even though they may not officially be the team leader.

According to the *Guide to the Project Management Body of Knowledge* (PMI, 2000), communication management in projects is the process required to ensure timely and appropriate generation,

The bigger the team, the more time must be spent on communication.

collection, dissemination, storage, and ultimately disposition of project information.

Communication Overhead

It may very well be that many projects get into trouble because no one realizes the amount of overhead time required for adequate communication. It is generally agreed that a typical individual can only deal with about seven to ten communication channels on a regular basis. This suggests that a project manager can only effectively communicate with seven to ten members of the team. However, the number of communication channels in a team is given by the equation

$$C = n(n-1)/2$$

where n is the number of team members (Sugimoto, 2002, p. 612). For ten members of the team (including the project manager), this yields 45 channels.

As the team grows above 10 members, the only way to handle communications is by increasing the administrative members of the team. This means that you begin to form a hierarchy, with intermediaries between the project manager and the team members. Sugimoto shows that when the team reaches 100 developers, you need 11 administrative people to handle communications.

What he does not address is the fact that, under this condition, the project manager no longer has direct contact with team members, since information flows to them through intermediaries. Thus, the quality of the information they receive (and disseminate) tends to degrade.

The point is that the bigger the team, the more time must be spent on communication, and this increases the administrative costs of the project.

Documentation

An important component of communication is documentation. My colleague, Janet Atkinson, suggests that you approach documentation as if you were facing litigation. I will leave it to you to ponder the implications of that suggestion.

> **Survival Tip:** Approach documentation as if you were facing litigation.

Here's a thought. Say you believed your company was doing something wrong, and you documented it. You might then be able to protect yourself in a lawsuit—but you might also get fired. However, the "Professional Responsibility" section of the PMBOK® lists the first task to be performed by a PMP® (Project Management Professional) as:

> *Ensure individual integrity and professionalism by adhering to legal requirements and ethical standards in order to protect the community and all stakeholders.*

This means that a project manager must be familiar with the laws that govern the project in the place where it is being conducted. This assumes, of course, that the project manager is truly the one in charge of the project. In that case, he or she is responsible

Change requests should always be documented so the project impact is minimized.

for everything in the project. In those organizations where the project manager's role is not so strong, then neither is the responsibility totally his or hers.

Change Requests

I include this under communication, although it could also be placed in a chapter discussing project control. Again, Janet suggests that you never accept a verbal change request. You must require that it be in writing. I would go so far as to say that you should also have a committee that approves such change requests, and that those approvals be in writing. The reason is very simple. Scope creep, which occurs when you accept requests for very small changes without requiring "payment" for them, will wreck a project. And furthermore, at the end of the job, everyone develops very convenient

> **Survival Tip:** Never accept verbal change requests.

amnesia—they don't remember any of the changes or the impact of those changes on the job. They just remember the original targets.

Here I believe project managers have a significant communication responsibility. When a request for a change is submitted, you must tell the person requesting the change precisely how it will impact the project. It may affect schedule, cost, or performance targets. Then ask if the person wants to accept that impact. You also must ensure that *all* stakeholders agree to the impact. Otherwise, the change request should be declined.

"Ostrich" Problems

Another communication problem that sometimes affects leaders is their handling of bad news. In his book, *On the Psychology of Military Incompetence,* author Norman Dixon (1984) cites anxiety as the most common cause of leadership failure. He identifies personal faults common to incompetence:

1. A fundamental conservatism and clinging to outworn tradition.
2. A tendency to reject or ignore information.
3. A tendency to underestimate the opponent.
4. Indecisiveness.
5. A failure to make use of surprise.
6. A predilection for frontal assaults.
7. A failure to make adequate reconnaissance.

Too often, incompetent leaders resist information because it might cause them to change their course of direction. The greater the impact of the new information, the more strenuously it is resisted because if changes must be made, then the persons involved were wrong before (Michaelson, 2001, p. 28).

While some of these personal characteristics do not apply to project managers, many do. The last one is especially appropriate—resisting information. Managers do not like bad news. They tend to adopt a "shoot the messenger" response, with the net result that people no longer inform them when something goes wrong. Clearly, you cannot solve problems you don't know about,

You can't solve problems you don't know about.

Have employees keep you informed about problem areas.

so you must urge people to tell you about problems as soon as they are discovered. Naturally, you encourage people to try to solve problems rather than dumping them on you. But you do need to be kept informed about those problems that are outside the routines of a person's job, so that you can assess the impact to the job and take the action needed to compensate for it.

> **Survival Tip:** Don't hide from bad news. Encourage people to tell you as soon as possible about extraordinary project problems so you can assess their impact and take steps to deal with them.

Keep the Boss and Sponsor Informed

Janet reminded me of another fundamental of management, but one that we sometimes forget—never let the boss or sponsor be surprised. In the same way that we sometimes resist listening to bad news, we also do not like to pass it on to our boss or sponsor.

I always told my people that they should tell me what they were doing to deal with problems. You should do the same when communicating bad news to your boss or sponsor. It's a big surprise to find out a few days before a project is supposed to be completed that it is going to be 13 weeks late

> **Survival Tip:** Don't ever let your boss or sponsor be surprised.

(as happened when the new Denver airport was built). This information should have been conveyed long before the deadline came that close!

MULALLY'S PRINCIPLES

Earlier in this chapter, I mentioned that Boeing adopted a new strategy to manage the 777 development program. They called it "Working Together" because it signified a very different approach than the old, throw-it-over-the-wall method that had typified past development projects. Because those

> **Survival Tip:** Adopt Mulally's principles to run your project. They are the keys to success.

principles were so effective, Alan Mulally, now President and CEO of Boeing Commercial Airplanes, still follows them in managing the company.

When I wrote to people asking for suggestions on how project managers can be effective, Alan wrote back:

> *News flash!!!!!!!!!!!!!! I have found our Working Together principles and practices to be the key to successful project management!!*

I agree with him. In fact, I wrote an entire book on the principles, explaining each one and making the case for its importance. Since that book, titled *Working Together* (Lewis, 2002), covers them in detail, I will simply list them here. I believe that all project managers must adopt these principles in order to succeed.

Compelling Vision

As I have already mentioned, a project needs a *compelling* vision—not a mundane idea, but one that excites people. A compelling vision energizes people and inspires them to persist in pursuing the goal even when the going gets rough. Don't underestimate the power of vision to give your team motivation that it would never have otherwise. Futurist Joel Barker's (1993) video, "Power of Vision," shows that great visions always precede great civilizations, successful individuals, and powerful companies. If you aren't yet convinced of the importance of vision, I suggest you view Barker's video.

Everyone Is Included

Remember that Dr. Phil's characteristics of people state that their number one concern is to be accepted and their number one fear is being rejected. It is common practice in organizations to exclude people from certain facets of a project. Only a small inner circle of people can have access to *privileged* information. This means that those who are excluded feel rejected. I don't believe you can have a successful team—or for that matter, any team at all—when some members of that team feel like outsiders. Yes, I know that some information must always be kept secret from the rest of the world, and yes, I know that some staff can't keep a secret. But most information and most staff don't fall into these categories.

Another aspect of this principle is that you include key suppliers on your project team. They then have a vested interest in providing excellent service to your company, and they can often contribute significantly to the project with good ideas.

Clear Performance Goals

Every member of the team must know what is expected of him or her—what, by when, and how much? Fuzzy goals lead to fuzzy outcomes. It is useful to set goals by asking two questions:

1. What is the desired outcome?
2. How will we know it has been achieved?

All team members must be aligned with the direction in which the project must move.

The outcome statement includes the vision and mission for each contributor, which, when achieved, will contribute to the overall project vision and mission. The second question defines how you will be able to tell the outcome has been achieved— whether quantitatively or qualitatively. This is sometimes called an *exit criteria*. Don't overlook the importance of exit criteria, since, if you can't tell if the project is actually completed, people may continue working on it endlessly.

One Plan

We know that no project can succeed if every person in the team goes his own way. All members must pull together—be aligned—with the direction in which the project must move. This is achieved by developing an integrated plan that defines each contributor's job. Each person or function may then have an individual plan, but it is part of the overall total project plan and there are no disconnects.

I have seen project plans for construction jobs in which there were no interdependencies shown between electrical and concrete work, so that one team was trying to do electrical work in the same area in which another crew was trying to pour concrete. Apparently, this kind of conflict is more common that you might think. It not only requires that you have *one* plan, but that it shows linkages between the different functions.

The Data Sets Us Free

If we know the facts about our situation, we are set free from speculation, fingerpointing, and fear. All too often, problems are stated in vague, emotion-laden terms. To illustrate this, in one of my seminars, I form small teams, present the following scenario, and ask each team how it would respond:

> *Imagine that you are a project team at Boeing and you receive a call from an engine manufacturer saying that they have just run a test on a new engine that is being designed for your airplane and that the engine blew up during the test. What do you do?*

They come up with some very good responses—mostly, alternatives to work around the problem so it won't delay the project. But seldom do they ask me what I mean when I say that the engine *blew up!* Did it literally explode? Did it quit running? Did it simply fail to meet its thrust requirements?

How can you solve a problem without knowing the facts that define it? Clearly, you cannot. Yet people attempt to do this every day.

You Can't Manage a Secret

It seems a common occurrence in projects that people know they have a problem but won't disclose it. They may tell themselves that they will first try to solve it before they tell anyone about it. After all, there's no need to get anybody excited unnecessarily. But when their attempts to solve the problem produce no results and begin to drag on, they grow even more afraid to tell because everyone will say, "Why didn't you tell us sooner?" So this approach often backfires.

In some organizations, admitting that you have a problem draws a shoot-the-messenger response, so there is no question why people don't tell that anything has gone wrong. Such a climate is not conducive to good performance of any kind, and managers who practice this approach do so without understanding that problems cannot be solved until they are first admitted and then defined.

People may go into denial because they fear rejection when they admit to having a problem. I have seen engineers do this. They think that having a problem means that they are somehow bad engineers. Nonsense! Technology is part science and part art. Problems are in the nature of the job. But tell that to the person who is afraid of being seen as a bad engineer, which could lead to his being rejected.

Whining Is Okay—Occasionally

It has long been conventional wisdom that you should keep emotions out of the workplace (at least negative emotions). Yet, managers want everyone to be motivated. It does not occur to them that *emotion* and *motivate* have a common root. Being motivated is to experience a highly positive emotional state. Essentially, you are told to leave negative emotions out of the job, but that it is okay to have positive ones.

Sorry, it doesn't work that way. People cannot segregate their emotions and experience only the positive ones. Besides, we know that negative feelings interfere with problem solving. When people are upset, they do not think rationally and objectively. In fact, there is a simple rule you must follow in dealing with problems:

Feelings → Facts → Solutions

Deal with feelings first. Let people vent a little. Then ask for the facts of the situation. Then move to solutions.

Propose a Plan, Find a Way

Sometimes when people are confronted with a really tough problem, they go into the "ain't-it-awful" mode and simply whine about their fate. Whining won't solve the problem, unfortunately. So my advice to them is: get the whining out of your system and tell me what you plan to do to solve your problem. Note that I didn't say, "Tell me how you're going to solve the problem." I said, "Tell me what you plan to do to solve your problem." What approach are you going to take? Does this approach require any resources that you don't presently have? I need to know such things so I can decide if you need help.

Listen to Each Other and Help Each Other

A team is a group of people who *work together* to achieve a common objective. Note that this requires collaboration and cooperation. Did you ever stop to think how rare it is to actually see a group function as a team?

Some years ago, I led a project team through a lessons-learned review following their achievement of a very important milestone. We listed all the factors that they felt had been done well and those they thought needed to be improved. Then they voted on the factors, and the number one factor that they felt contributed to their success was, "We actually worked as a team." They cooperated, helped each other, communicated well, and were excited about the challenge of the job.

Sadly, the more common scenario is turf battles, secrecy, competition, and in-fighting. It's no wonder that such projects have difficulty meeting their targets.

Emotional Resilience

I wrote about this earlier in the chapter, so I won't go over it at length again here. Let's just say that good project managers "roll with the punches," and when they get knocked down, they get up and keep on fighting.

Have Fun—Enjoy the Journey and Each Other

This is the last of Mulally's principles and one that research shows is very important. People who enjoy their work and their team mates are more creative and productive than those who do not. I have been told that work is not supposed to be fun ("that's why it's called work"), but this is simply false. If your work isn't fun, it won't be very motivating. And if you dislike the people you work with, you certainly won't function as a true team.

One Final Principle

Alan tells me that since I wrote *Working Together,* he has added a new principle. He calls it "People First." Rosen (1996) claims that when managers are asked about the most important factor that distinguishes a successful company, they typically say that people are the most valuable resource. But when asked to rank a list of ten factors, *people* rank somewhere around five or six. This is an example of what Argyris (1990) called one's theory espoused versus theory-in-use: Respondents espoused the theory that people are their most valuable resource, but they practiced a very different belief.

When you think about it, you will realize that it is not the building and technology that make you money. It is the people that occupy the building and apply the technology that enrich the company. In fact, it is very important to state it this way: *Projects are people!* And the core of project management is dealing with people. Technology is secondary.

6

How to Handle Unreasonable Demands

*I*n today's high-speed, high-stress work environment, project managers often find themselves under huge pressure to deliver results without being given adequate resources to meet the targets. How they handle these demands can make or break them.

Because no one of us can have all of the answers to all situations, I asked a number of colleagues to contribute some suggestions that I can share with you, and these follow in

> *I have learned that anybody can handle smooth water, but that the people who succeed do so consistently and know how to stay afloat when storms are raging.*
>
> — Phillip McGraw

Project managers often work under huge pressure to stay afloat and deliver results.

this chapter. First, however, I think it is important that all of us are on the same page.

A common expression in project management is, "Good, fast, cheap—pick two." These are known as the triple constraints on a project. However, this approach combines scope and performance, and they are not the same thing.

Performance refers to technical requirements or qualitative aspects, or simply put, what must the *deliverable* do for the customer? Scope refers to the magnitude or size of the job: How much work must be done to deliver the desired result? All kinds of combinations are possible. For example, you can have a job that is huge but does not have very stringent performance requirements. A property development project might fall into this category. On the other hand, you can have a relatively small project (in terms of duration, number of people involved, or whatnot) that has extremely high performance requirements. An example is retinal surgery.

In addition to the performance and scope targets are cost and time. How much will it cost to complete the project according to

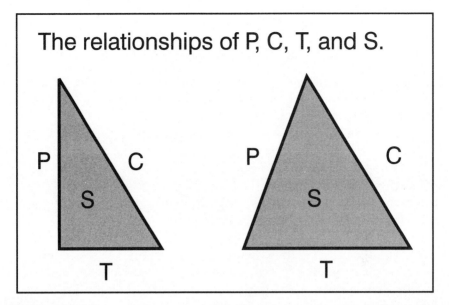

Figure 6.1
Triangle Showing PCTS

the requirements? And how long will it take (time)? The relationship between these four variables can be expressed by the following formula:

$$C = f(P, T, S)$$

In words, the formula states, "Cost is a function of performance, time, and scope." Ideally, it could be written as an exact mathematical expression, but in fact we are often estimating the values of the variables and so are unable to do this.

The relationship can be further demonstrated by an analogy, using a triangle, as shown in Figure 6.1. In this figure, the sides are equivalent to P, C, and T, while the area is equivalent to S.

From geometry, you will remember that if you know the lengths of the three sides,

> **Survival Tip: Don't let anyone dictate all four variables or project objectives. They can dictate three, but you must specify the fourth!**

you can calculate the area (S). Or, if you know the area and the lengths of two sides, you can calculate the length of the third side. However, you cannot *arbitrarily* assign values to all four variables—

if they fit, it is completely by accident! Yet this is exactly what senior managers and/or project sponsors attempt. It is, in fact, one of the top ten most common causes of project failure.

The common scenario is for the project manager to receive the P, T, and S requirements for a job, and to then spend time estimating its cost. When this cost is conveyed to senior managers, however, they have a heart attack. They do not believe your numbers; they are certain that by pressuring you they can get you to confess that large amounts of padding inflate the cost figure. With a little extra cleverness on your part, you can remove the "fat" and trim costs significantly. So they dictate the project budget to you on the spot, or they threaten to find someone who can do it for less. Unfortunately, senior managers are sometimes right. Project teams do get carried away trying to protect themselves sometimes, and they do inject excessive padding to ensure that they can meet the targets to which they commit themselves. The problem with this approach to planning is that excessive padding will price a product out of the market. If the job has been justified based upon a specified return-on-investment figure, all that padding could scuttle it. Furthermore, padding that is built into the budget, if approved, *will be spent*! This is an example of Parkinson's Law: Work always expands to fit the time (or the budget) allowed.

It is a project manager's responsibility to ensure that padding covers risk only and is not excessive. The problem is that you can't always tell by how much your team's numbers are padded. So you must make all of them aware of financial realities. Furthermore, the company must remove

> **Survival Tip:** You should ensure that padding covers risk only and that it is not excessive.

any penalties for small variances that affect a project, as all activities vary and zero variance is impossible.

Assuming you have quoted a realistic cost figure, if the sponsor or other manager complains that it is too high, respond by asking what he wants to cut from the right side of the equation. The equation must balance, after all. Usually it is the scope that is cut. Increasing time slightly may not reduce costs, and trying to reduce time dramatically usually drives costs higher, as shown in Figure 6.2.

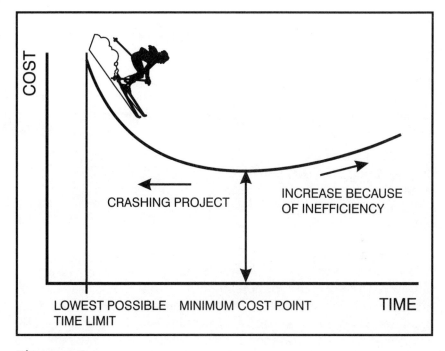

Figure 6.2
Time-Cost Tradeoff

In addition, reducing performance requirements to reduce cost is not usually an acceptable option. Reducing scope may be your only recourse.

There is a way to reduce scope that is sometimes possible in a hardware or software development project. That is to remove some of the features of the product (using the word generically to mean software or hardware). Smith and Reinertsen (1995) have shown that each feature added to a product increases the complexity (and therefore the cost) significantly. Each new element added nearly doubles complexity. That relationship is represented by the formula:

$$N = \Sigma n! / [(n-i)! i!]$$

where N is the number of potential interactions and n is the number of elements. Also, the summation is from i=2 to n.

As Smith and Reinertsen point out, the "do-everything" project is an enormous trap, into which many clever people fall. To avoid the trap, a company must develop an incremental innovation

99

approach—but this approach will never be as popular as the do-everything project. From an economic standpoint, however, it can be shown to be far superior to innovate incrementally than to attempt everything at once.

> **Survival Tip: Beware the "do-everything" project! Show stakeholders the tradeoffs possible by reducing features.**

In any case, a project manager should understand these tradeoffs so that they can be recommended to project sponsors or other senior managers when there are not enough resources to do everything. However, be sure to back up your recommendations with data: When all you have to offer is an opinion about how long things will take or how much a job will cost, you have very little credibility with managers who outrank you. And in those situations you usually lose the debate. Again, one of your best survival strategies is to practice sound project management methods.

> **Survival Tip: Your plan must always be in writing!**

As Michaelson (2001) has written, "If your plan is not in writing, you do not have a plan at all. Instead, you have only a dream, a vision, or perhaps even a nightmare" (p. 3).

SUGGESTIONS FROM ASSOCIATES

As I was working on this book, I decided to survey some of my associates for suggestions about dealing with unreasonable demands. Following is the note I sent to them:

> *Hi Everyone:*
>
> *I am working on another book, and have a question for all of you. I frequently am asked by seminar participants what to do when you give a senior manager an estimate for how long a project will take and what it will cost, and they tell you that's too long and too expensive. "You should be able to do it for less," they say. And they refuse to listen to any counter-argument. I have my own ideas about this, but would like to draw on your varied experience,*

as I expect most of you have encountered similar situations. Clearly, a project manager needs a variety of possible responses, and your thoughts would be very helpful. I will also credit you in the book.

It is not a problem dealing with a reasonable person—the question is, how do you deal with one who insists on being unreasonable.

Thanks in advance for sharing your thoughts with me.

Response from Adrian Warner

This is a common "emotional" response. Our management environment used to encourage overloading the schedule (still does to some extent) and

> *I have known Adrian for about 10 years. He is a senior manager with a large electronics company.*

then taking out features as time schedules slipped. This permeated throughout the organization at all levels. It was done in the divine belief that more was done with an overloaded schedule because it forced people to "work harder."

When I came here one of my first steps was to train every Technical Lead that reported to me in negotiation techniques—we used the Karass course. Then we brought you in to provide the project management skills. This taught my team that there are three primary variable resources, cost, time frame, and scope. Usually the resources are constrained, and normally the time frame is as well—even if it is one that is driven by emotion rather than reason. Thus, in conclusion, the real variable is scope—how much can we do in the allotted time frame?

> **Survival Tip:** Benchmark other organizations to find out how long it takes them to do work similar to yours.

Keeping good benchmarks on your organization's productivity/performance and that of other industrial organizations can be a powerful ace card to hold. Depending on the relationship between the Project Manager and the Senior Executive, and their own personal styles, it may be possible to challenge the manager's assumption that your

Keep good benchmarks on your organization's productivity and performance.

team is not performing (as implied.) First I would push for the factual basis for the statement. Often it is, "Ten years ago we built project X, in Y months." Further, the same statement has often been made many times before. If it has, determine the truth. Almost certainly this legendary achievement is not as grand as it has been made out.

This is especially true of companies that grow from entrepreneurial roots. I saw this at [a computer company]. The company had grown from a successful start-up in the city center of [a large city] with nearly 50 employees to an organization of 800 employees in four years. As the company grew, the projects tended to become less and less deterministic and more prone to slippage. Over time, the original property (where the company started out) gained a mythical significance inside the company, to the

> **Survival Tip:** Find out the facts about legendary projects and challenge them should they prove to be false.

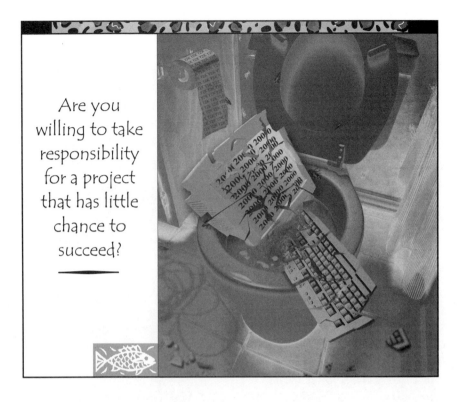

Are you willing to take responsibility for a project that has little chance to succeed?

point where a small project team was actually set up at that address. There was no success, and there is no "magic" location. Management forgot that when they were small they did not document products, that manufacturing was done by small entrepreneurial companies, and the product quality sucked. Our customers—a small band of innovative enthusiasts—tolerated it in the beginning. When the product hit prime time all that had to change.

Against this backdrop, I led a team that developed a new disk interface product in a record 16 weeks—from design to manufacture. It was done with teamwork, high re-use of available technology within the company, and tight communication. Oh, and it was done in the new facility—so much for magic!

Returning to your question. As soon as you start justifying your plan, you adopt a defensive position; in effect, you have already lost. Further, if you present a plan to management that is not optimal and does not achieve the objective, you're dead. Situations like this demand:

1. A watertight plan, with reasonable mitigation (aggression may be used to sell the plan, but better not be the basis of the plan, or it will likely fail).
2. Don't accept assertions without data—find the truth behind the legend of the company's historical successes.
3. Treat these situations as a negotiation.

In the end, if you are in an impossible situation, with unreasonable people, maybe you are working for the wrong organization! I hope these thoughts help.

Response from George Hollins

George is another longtime friend. He is director of design and construction for a large university.

This has practically become part of our routine now—with the tougher economic times and all.

We now provide an *ala carte* listing of items that can be cut from the project, and their respective costs. The Vice President can selectively cut based on estimates of the various items. We have to spend planning money to develop the project far enough for the estimates.

With regard to schedule, it pretty much is what it is. We can do some adjusting by paralleling work and adding a limited amount of resources. We have a very good historic record of how much work can be accomplished in a given period of time. Pushing the envelope beyond this historic data generally results in failure. We proved this on a major project within the last two years. This validated our message. We've become believable—we're not good at telling lies.

Hope this helps!

> **Survival Tip: Provide** stakeholders with a cost-tradeoff list, so that they can choose those items they consider essential and drop the others.

Response from Barry Briggs

Working within a large company, your possibilities are limited. Generally, my approach was to go back to the drawing board and try to break down the project into units. If it was a new venture, I would try to break the investment into reve-

Barry has been a friend and my web site developer for a number of years. Since he has done a number of projects for me, I consider him to be an excellent source of practical ideas.

nue streams with a base cost of the venture and additional costs for each revenue stream with expected revenue. Then I would go back and say, "OK we can reduce the cost but we will have to give up this and this, which will reduce the potential revenue by whatever."

I would do the same with internal capital expenditures and projects if they were revenue producing or cost saving.

So it then comes down to, which cost saving or revenue stream do you want to cut, basically turning the decision to cut the cost (and the loss of revenue or cost savings) back on them. Most of the time that made the difference. Few want to be the decision maker that cut a potential revenue stream or cost savings.

Pricing a development project is much the same. Our clients always want *everything* for *a little cost!* I now do most cost projections on custom development based on the core code (the minimum to get the job done), and then I add costs for each "feature." If the price is too high, I can immediately begin to offer reduced pricing by cutting "features." This way, the customer controls the cost of the project by deciding which features are necessary to the success of the project.

As with everything in life, however, you sometimes have to just pull the plug. If there is no reasoning with the person who has control, you have to

> **Survival Tip:** You sometimes have to just pull the plug.

draw the line. Are you willing to take the responsibility for a project that you know is underfunded and has little chance of successful completion? In my case, I am not. When with the "unnamed" larger company, I gave the decision-maker a letter declining leadership of the project and clearly stated that I did not think that the project had much chance of success given the budget constraints. I couldn't, in good faith to the company, start a project that I felt would ultimately result in harm to the company.

I don't work there anymore. I was not fired, but after that I was no longer the wonder boy that could do anything. In due time I just "left to pursue other goals."

It is not a decision that I regret. In fact, if faced with the same decision today, it wouldn't take me as long to get around to writing the letter. I have less patience with ignorance these days.

In my current position [as the owner of his own business], when I feel a potential client is cutting the project to the point that it has little chance of success, I will drop the project. While I'm in this business to make a living, I'm not in the business *just* to make a living. I also want to create successful products. I have no desire to be associated with projects that fail because of something that I allowed to happen. If it fails, I want to make sure that I did everything in my power to make it successful.

> **Survival Tip: When you have a choice, don't take on projects that have almost no chance of success to begin with.**

My only regret is that I don't have enough time to "donate" to good ideas. Sometimes the ideas are great, but there is just not enough financing to make it work.

It's something I can look forward to when I get "rich."

Hope this helps.

My Own Suggestions

I often tell people in my seminars that they always have four choices when they find themselves in a bad situation. They are:

1. Change the situation (always the preferred choice).
2. Change how you feel about it.
3. Leave.
4. Maintain the status quo.

If the manager you are dealing with is not highly unreasonable, you may be able to change his or her opinion. Sometimes the person will be persuaded by a good argument. Perhaps good data will do it. Or you may have to ask, "What do I need to do to convince you that the project targets can't be met?" There are two possible responses. One is, "You can't convince me." When you get that as the first response, you should ask, "Really? There's absolutely nothing I can do?" If the person is adamant, then you take one of the remaining four choices. The other response is that the individual does tell you what you must do to—and if you can do it, then the battle is half won.

A manager may say that there is no way he'll be convinced not because he is being unreasonable, but simply because he doesn't know what it will take. In that case, you may choose your second option: Change your feelings about the situation. This means that you do the best you can to cope, but without getting an ulcer over it. This is an acceptable choice *if* you can actually change how you feel. But be careful. It is easy to fool yourself into thinking you aren't bothered, when actually your feelings are gnawing away at you. This is sure to cause you trouble later on.

When you are dealing with a super-macho, totally unreasonable manager, you have to decide if you are willing to change your feelings or whether you are going to leave the situation (as was suggested by two of my friends). Sometimes, it just isn't worth it. Who wants to play a rigged game forever?

Please note that the fourth option—maintaining the status quo—should be considered only a temporary one. If you stay in a bad situation for a long time and are being constantly upset by it, you will suffer mental and physical problems. You owe it to yourself not to remain in such a situation for an extended time.

INFLUENCING OTHERS

Often when you tell a manager that something can't be done, a couple of things happen. One, you frustrate that manager's concern for achieving some business objective. Two, you may appear uncooperative, or lacking a "can-do" attitude. In either case,

Conflict often occurs when one party frustrates the concerns of another.

Learn to say "no" in the appropriate way.

the manager attempts to reassert her authority, and you get into a conflict.

Conflict occurs when one party frustrates the concerns of another; these concerns include objectives, values, beliefs, interests, and so on. So the very fact that you appear to be placing a barrier in the way of achieving her objectives causes the manager to see you as being difficult. For that reason, it is very important that you say "no" in the appropriate way.

Notice that all of my associates suggested ways of offering the sponsor (or client, or whoever) a set of tradeoffs. Most of us are aware that we can't always have everything for the price we can afford, so being very clear about feature-cost tradeoffs is a good strategy.

You may also find the following opening line to be effective in avoiding a conflict: "My team and I have looked carefully at all of the project objectives, and if you want us to achieve all of them, here is what we are going to need (in the way of money, resources, etc.). If these resources are not available, we suggest that some tradeoffs are possible to keep us in line with what is available." Such a statement makes it clear that you want to act in the best interests of the organization, that you recognize certain limitations that must be addressed and are asking the sponsor to make some choices.

In any case, what is of real importance here is that you understand some basic principles of dealing with people. I want to suggest three books that are invaluable in this respect: Stephen Covey's (1989) *7 Habits of Highly Effective People;* Phillip McGraw's (1999) *Life Strategies;* and Cialdini's (1993) *Influence: The Power of Persuasion.* Allow me to share some thoughts from McGraw's book:

> *In every strategy involving people, there are always at least two things you must do: You must overcome their resistances and excuses, and then get them to accept your view of the world (1999, p. 47).*

However, you cannot do this without understanding the person you are dealing with. Dr. Phil goes on to say:

> *You must understand someone and know what makes them tick before you can connect with them. They need to see similarities between you and your values and their own. That is the basis of bonding (1999, p. 47).*

This comment immediately sheds light on why some project managers have difficulty communicating with their bosses. They do not seem to share the values of the boss. Remember that I told you that you must think business when you become a project manager—you must think in terms of economics. Often, technologists (engineers, scientists, programmers) become project managers and it becomes clear to everyone that they still think in terms of technology—they have no clear understanding of business realities. These individuals have a hard time convincing their more business-oriented bosses that something can't be done, because they are often perceived as perfectionists who don't know how to finish any undertaking.

To continue with Dr. Phil's statement that you must understand the person you're dealing with, he offers the following suggestions. At a minimum, he says, he wants to know:

1. *What do they value the most in their lives: Are ethics a big deal? Do money and success define them? Do they value strength, or compassion? What really matters in their outlook on life?*
2. *What are their experiences and beliefs about how life does and should work?*
3. *What resistances or predispositions—fears, biases, prejudices—do they have?*
4. *What positions or approaches or philosophies are they most likely to reject or accept?*
5. *What do they need to hear from a person in order to conclude that that person is fundamentally "okay" and to be trusted?*
6. *What sorts of things do they consider relevant?*
7. *What do they want most in their lives? (1999, p. 48).*

A couple of observations are in order. For many managers, number three above is very important. Managers often fear loss of control. When you tell a manager that something can't be done, you immediately trigger this fear. That's why it's important to offer tradeoffs—it signals that control can be maintained.

Also, point number five is very important. It substantiates what I said about project managers talking the language of economics, and it tells upper management that you have business interests foremost on your mind. Unless they see you as "one of them," you will not be trusted and will therefore have no credibility.

7

Out of the Crisis

*P*rojects often run into trouble. As Murphy's Law states, whatever can go wrong will go wrong. And, as someone has said, Murphy was an optimist!

Almost anyone can lead a project that is proceeding smoothly. It is when a crisis develops that a project manager is put to the test. And it is not what happens, but how you react to it that will determine how others will measure you.

> **Survival Tip:** It is not what happens, but how you react to it that will determine how others measure you.

Human beings have several common reactions to stress. In denial, the person pretends things aren't really that bad.

I call this "ostrich" management.

EMOTIONAL RESILIENCE

In a conversation with Alan Mulally, who is presently CEO and President of Boeing commercial airplanes, he said that a consultant once told him that his job was to set the context, the climate for the 777 project (Alan was chief engineer of the 777 program at the time). The consultant said, "If you fall down on the floor kicking and screaming when there is a problem, then everyone in the team will think the project is falling apart." For this reason, Alan says a project manager needs emotional resilience.

It's not whether you get knocked down; it's whether you get up.
— Vince Lombardi

In fact, in an e-mail that I received from him just a few days before this was written, he told me that due to the decline in airplane sales that resulted from the aftermath of 9/11, Boeing has reduced its staff from 127,000 to 64,000 and cut production of airplanes from 48 to 24 a month. But, he said, he was proud to serve at this unprecedented time.

That is the attitude of a leader. A person lacking in emotional resilience would be playing "ain't it awful," lamenting his or her misfortune and complaining about all of the unfortunate events that were making life difficult. There is no doubt that Boeing is going through some of the toughest times in its history. The events of 9/11 crippled the airline industry. Airlines can't buy planes when the public stops flying. Now, as I write this, we are in the sixth day of the war with Iraq, the airlines have reported a drop of 30 to 40 percent in international travel, and United is on the brink of complete collapse.

It would be easy to wallow in self-pity at this time, but Boeing managers have done what must be done to ensure the survival of the company. They have performed tough surgery—and still remain upbeat.

As the sayings go, "No storm can last forever," and "This too shall pass."

REACTIONS TO STRESS

Human beings tend to have several common reactions to stress. These include denial, blaming others, and problem solving. In denial, the person tries to pretend that things really aren't as bad as they seem. I call this "ostrich" management—stick your head in a hole in the ground and pretend nothing bad is happening. Of course, you cannot, by ignoring a problem, expect it to be solved or to go away. The long-term result is that the problem grows out of bounds and finally can no longer be ignored. What might have been a minor issue when it first appeared is now a crisis.

Blaming others is another common response. It is incompetent staff who are at fault, or advisors who gave the manager bad advice. Or it is the war with Iraq or a bad economy or Al Qaida. It may even be true, but spending all your time blaming others will not solve the problem.

The problem-solving response is the healthy one. It doesn't matter who caused the crisis or why it happened. The question is,

Hope is not a strategy.

———

Wishful thinking doesn't solve problems.

what can be done about it. Effective leaders step up to the plate, stand up straight, and tell their followers that together they will survive the crisis and be stronger for it. This is what Mayor Giuliani did in the moments after the World Trade Center collapsed on 9/11. And for many New Yorkers, it was the first time they perceived Giuliani as a true leader.

HOPE IS NOT A STRATEGY

In his best-selling book, *Who Moved My Cheese?*, Dr. Spencer Johnson (1998) describes two little people and two mice that go out each day in search of cheese. They must find the cheese in a maze, and they are successful. Life is good for a while. Every day they go to the source of cheese and have their fill of it. Then disaster strikes! The cheese does not appear in the usual spot. Someone has moved the cheese!

The mice quickly abandon the old spot and go off looking for cheese in other parts of the maze. The little people, however, continue returning to the same old spot, lamenting that someone has moved their cheese and hoping that it will return.

Hope, however, is not an effective strategy for solving the moved-cheese problem. As Dr. Phil (1999) says, "Life rewards action." Not intentions. Not hope. Action.

> **Survival Tip: When life hands you a lemon, make lemonade!**

Because they took action, the mice eventually found the new source of cheese. They adapted to the change. The little people simply wallowed in self-pity and went hungry, claiming that life was unfair and that they were victims.

I see this all the time in projects. As a matter of fact, too many project managers are passive, rather than proactive.

> *Life rewards action. Not intentions, action!*
> — Dr. Phillip McGraw

They wait until a problem develops before doing anything about it. Rather than practice prevention, they practice surgery or apply tourniquets to stop the hemorrhaging. It is far better to prevent a disease than to have to cure it!

This is, in fact, a major reason for post-mortem or lessons-learned reviews. Once we know what caused an accident, we can use that knowledge to keep the same thing from happening—we hope. The problem is that teams don't hold lessons-learned reviews for projects as they should, so you

> **Survival Tip: It is better to prevent a disease than to have to cure it.**

see the same mistakes being repeated. As the old adage has it, if you don't learn from history, you are doomed to repeat it.

Remember Mulally's principle—propose a plan, find a way? As a project manager, especially, this is what is expected of you. Whining may be okay—just to get it off your chest—but you better start figuring out what to do and quit hoping the problem will go away, because that never happens. Restating Murphy's Law in

When things go
wrong it is human
nature to want to
blame someone.

———

But if you admit
to mistakes, you
can move on
quickly.

terms of chance: There is a far greater probability that things will
accidentally go wrong than that they will accidentally go right.

BLAME AND PUNISHMENT

When things go wrong, it seems to be human nature to want to
blame someone. In the first edition of my book, *Project Planning,
Scheduling, and Control* (Lewis, 1991), I told the story of a Japanese
pilot named Captain Asoh, who landed a DC 8 in perfect compass
alignment with the runway, but in San Francisco Bay. He did so
very skillfully, I might add. So skillfully that many passengers
didn't realize anything was wrong until they noticed that they
were in the water, on the same level as nearby boats!

The passengers were all rescued, there were no serious injuries
or casualties, and the plane was even recovered. Of course, it is always true of a situation like this that we want to know the cause,
so that future accidents can be prevented. Therefore, an inquest

was held. Notice that "inquest" is the root of the word *inquisi-tion*—and the purpose of inquisitions is not just to get to the truth, but also to punish the guilty.

At the inquest, the chief examiner asked, "Captain Asoh, can you tell us how you managed to land your plane, in perfect alignment with the runway, in San Francisco Bay?"

The room was silent as everyone awaited the Captain's defense. After a moment, he said, "Well, as you Americans like to say, I screwed up."

That was it. The inquisition was over. Rather than deny responsibility (as was expected), Captain Asoh simply admitted that he made a mistake. The fault was his and his alone. Lesson learned: Don't land your plane in San Francisco Bay, even if you are perfectly aligned with the runway. Another lesson learned: If you screw up, just admit it. It's much less painful than having everyone beat up on you anyway.

In fact, this has become known as Asoh's defense—simply admit you made a mistake and get on with your life. You must, of course, accept the consequences of your mistake. And here is where we make a bad situation worse. We want to avoid the consequences of our mistakes, so we try to pass the blame on to someone or something else. The instruments malfunctioned. The devil made me do it (to use comedian Flip Wilson's line). It was an act of God (He gets blamed for a lot of things—like building in a flood plain, then getting washed away). Or you had bad neighbors. Or grew up poor. Or whatever.

Administering blame and punishment does not solve problems! It may make you feel better, but you are still left with the problem.[1] Only a problem-solving approach will solve a problem. This means that only two questions are actually important at this point:

1. What caused the problem?
2. What can be done to solve it?

---

[1] I'm not saying that people actually guilty of a crime, malpractice, or irresponsible behavior should not be punished. I'm simply saying this should not be your primary focus in general.

SOLVING PROJECT PROBLEMS

There are four things you can do when a project hits a pothole. Only four. They are:

1. If it is a very small pothole, just ignore it and drive on.
2. Solve the problem without changing the plan.
3. Change the plan to get around the pothole.
4. Cancel the project.

Notice that these responses progress from minor to major steps. Canceling a project is about the most serious step you can take, but sometimes it is necessary.

Let's address these in order and think about what they mean.

Ignore It

When a project deviates from plan a small amount, and there is no indication that a trend is developing (that is, the project is drifting progressively off course), the prudent thing to do is ignore the deviation. After all, processes *will* vary—holding to a zero variance from plan is not only foolish, but impossible. The question is how much tolerance you can maintain. For well-defined construction projects, the possible tolerance may be only ± 5 percent. For type IV projects, the tolerances may be very large—as much as minus 25 percent to plus 100 percent.

The trick is to stay alert to trends. If a project drifts off target progressively for several reporting periods in a row, it is a sign that you must intervene to bring it back on track.

Solve the Problem

Clearly, it is preferable to solve the problem quickly, without having to change the plan. Here are a few things you might do to solve the problem:

1. Replace a low-performing person with a high-performing one.

2. Change a process. For example, if you are painting a wall with a brush and it is going too slowly, start spray painting.

3. Remove the cause of the problem.

Change the Plan

Sometimes none of these tactics will work, and you simply have to revise your plan. Examples of these changes would be:

1. Add more resources. This means, effectively, that you increase the cost of the job. If you don't

   Turkish proverb: No matter how far you've gone on the wrong road, turn around!

   have more people to put on the job, you may have to ask your existing team members to work overtime. This is not a long-term remedy, however, because fatigue will soon eat into any gain in output that you achieve.

2. Reduce project scope. This may mean eliminating some feature from a product, or deferring some part of the work until later (such as painting a wall instead of using wallpaper, since painting is faster).

3. Paralleling or overlapping project activities, so that they are no longer sequential. This may be done to regain a slip in schedule. However, it may also increase errors, resulting in more rework, and can actually backfire because the rework puts you back where you started.

4. Accept that the project cannot meet its original targets and revise the plan to reflect current reality.

Cancel the Project

This is always traumatic, but sometimes it is the best thing to do. This is especially true in failing product development projects, so you can deploy your resources to another job that will be profitable.

Sioux Indian proverb: When you're riding a dead horse, dismount!

Have the good judgment to ask for help before project failure occurs.

ASK FOR HELP!

Heaven forbid that you do this! I know. Asking for help is admitting that you aren't up to the job, that you have failed. Everyone will reject you if you do this.

Maybe. But they *will* certainly reject you later on if the project fails, when it could have been saved had you swallowed your pride and asked someone for advice. As I've said, life is full of potholes, and every so often you hit one that you don't know how to deal with. That is why CEOs have boards of directors. It is why the president has a cabinet. None of these people can have all the answers, so they rely on experts to advise them when they hit an obstacle. Why not do the same yourself? Assemble a board of advisors—people

> **Survival Tip:** Find a few colleagues who will be willing to act as your board of advisors. Draw on their expertise when you are up against a situation you aren't sure how to handle.

It is fine to have advisors give you solutions, but you must learn the principles behind the solutions.

Don't become a lifelong dependent.

you respect, who have experience outside your own, and who are willing to help you through the rough times!

You may be surprised to learn that, rather than seeing you as weak, people will see you as having the good judgment to know when you are outside your element and need someone else's advice. And your advisors will be flattered that you value their input.

I have learned over the years that everyone likes to have others draw on their expertise, so long as you don't become a leech. I have occasionally had people write me for advice, and when I gave it, they sent

> **Survival Tip: You must learn the principles and laws that govern things, so you can apply them in solving problems.**

me a flurry of requests to solve all of their problems. After a time, I quit responding; not only do I lack the time to solve someone else's problems (I hardly have time to deal with my own), but the only way to really help someone is to teach that person to help himself. If you continue to assist him, you create a lifelong dependent.

This should give you something to think about. It's fine to have your advisors give you solutions, but if you don't learn the *principles* behind the solutions, you will become that lifelong dependent I just mentioned.

I find it difficult to get this across to people. For several years, I taught a seminar entitled "Dealing with Difficult Employees." I developed this program because, in my own management experience, I had never known a manager who didn't have a difficult employee. And I struck gold. My audiences always overflowed the room. People were eager to find answers to dealing with their "problem children." But in fact, I soon learned, they *really* wanted me to tell them what to do with Charlie or with Linda—specifically! Right then and there, on the spot! They had no interest in learning principles.

Yet, all education is really based on principles and examples of how to apply them. Once you know the method, the nature of the specific case doesn't matter, you apply your principle to it. Electrical engineers are taught Ohm's Law. Once they know it, they apply it to so many things. Mechanical engineers learn the laws of physics (such as the law of inertia); these, too, can be applied to many different situations. Nurses learn the principles involved in treating infections, or in stopping bleeding, or cleaning a wound, and use them daily.

Defining the Problem

One of Dr. Phil's life laws is, you either get it or you don't. I am convinced that many people simply don't get it when it comes to problem solving. Mainly, they don't get that the way you define the problem affects how you solve it, and it is therefore exceedingly important that you define the problem correctly before you try to solve it. This is substantiated in Rule 15, from a document entitled *100 Rules for NASA Project Managers* (NASA, 1996):

> *The seeds of problems are laid down early. Initial planning is the most vital part of a project. The review of most failed projects or project problems indicate the disasters were* well planned to happen *from the start (p. 2, emphasis added).*

This also verifies my contention that about 80 percent of projects that fail do so at the outset because they have not been defined properly. We always are convinced that we know the problem to be solved. All we need do is solve it.

> **Survival Tip: Be sure you properly define the problem to be solved before attempting to solve it.**

But this "ready-fire-aim" approach usually leads to disaster. Part of the reason for our tendency to react this way might lie with our education system. We are taught to be problem solvers, not problem definers. The definition is provided; all we are required to do is produce a solution.

In a book called *Exploring Requirements,* authors Gause and Weinberg (1989) offer a simple example: Build a dwelling that will protect humans from a hostile environment. Figure 7.1 shows some potential solutions.

All options are wholly valid solutions to the problem *as stated.* Clearly, the difficulty lies in the interpretation of key words— hostile environment, dwelling, protect—and words that aren't included. How many humans? How big are they? Protect from what aspects of the hostile environment? Wolves, temperature, vacuum?

If you had given this problem to NASA engineers to solve, they may well have built the space station pictured in Figure 7.1. Had the team been Eskimos, they may have designed the igloo. From tribes living in the African jungle, where wild animals are a threat, you would have received a different interpretation. Remember, we filter everything through our models of the world.

Solutions in Search of Problems

Related to this difficulty of defining problems is the solution in search of a problem. This is the pitfall in using consultants to help solve organizational problems. Consultants usually come from specialized

> *When all you have is a hammer, everything looks like a nail.*

backgrounds, such as sales, finance, engineering, organization

Four possibilities
for a dwelling.

Figure 7.1
Solutions to the Dwelling Problem

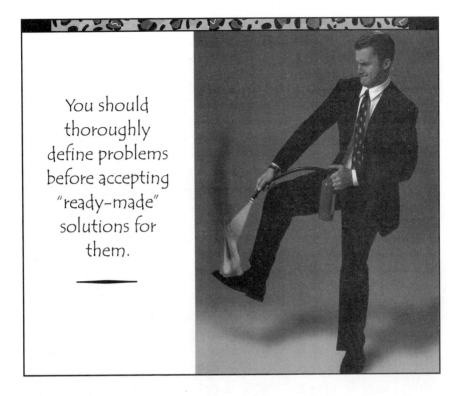

You should thoroughly define problems before accepting "ready-made" solutions for them.

development, or team building. Because of their specialized expertise, they tend to define problems to fit their solutions. If a team is experiencing conflict, they do a team-building intervention—perhaps taking the entire team to a ropes course, where they must physically overcome various obstacles and can only do so if they help each other. If the problem is financial, then a sales consultant will try to improve sales, a financial analyst consultant will examine the books, an organization development expert consultant will try to restructure the company, and so on.

> **Survival Tip:** Be cautious of experts. They are likely to try to solve every problem with the same "hammer."

This malady affects not only consultants, but people within the organization as well. My advice that you thoroughly define a problem before you let anyone try to solve it is based on both our ready-fire-aim tendencies and our inclination to apply the same solution to every problem.

PARTING WORDS

In closing this chapter, there is one more of the 100 NASA rules that I think you should probably frame and hang in your office. It is Rule 6:

> *A comfortable project manager is one waiting for his next assignment or one on the verge of failure. Security is not normal to project management (op cit., p. 1).*

So, now that I have you completely depressed—you can call me for a counseling appointment! Hi.

8

Your Self-Development Plan

*A*s is true of managing a project, you can't get there until you know where "there" is. You must decide on your goal or mission. Do you want to be a career project manager, or just remain an accidental one? If you want to be a world-class (career) project manager, then you have to "go for broke" and develop *all* of your skills. If you're content to just survive for the short term, then you should be able to do that by practicing the suggestions in this book while avoiding those situations that require more skills than you already possess.

To construct a self-development plan (SDP), you should treat it like a project—which it is. The steps involved are: 1. Define your mission and vision; 2. Develop a strategy or overall game plan to get you there; 3. Develop a detailed tactical or implementation plan that will achieve the strategy; 4. Start working on it, monitor

127

You can't get there until you know where "there" is.

———

You must decide on your goal or mission.

your progress, and make corrections as you go (execution and control); and 5. Enjoy the result!

1. MISSION AND VISION

Vision always precedes mission. Your vision defines the final outcome you are trying to achieve. I like to say that it defines "done." It is a concept or image in mind of the outcome, and when you achieve it, you have reached your destination. The clearer the vision in your mind's eye, the more likely you are to achieve it. If you want to develop your ability to visualize your desired outcomes, I recommend Shakti Gawain's book, *Creative Visualization* (2002). One way to flesh out your vision is to think in terms of the things you *must have, want to have,* and those that would be *nice to have* as an end result. Then concentrate on the must-haves and wants, and don't worry too much about the nice-to-have list.

Assess
Yourself

Any gap
between where
you are and
where you
want to be is a
developmental
need.

It is important to understand that a fuzzy vision won't work. For example, if you would like to be a world-class project manager, what does that mean? What kind of skills would you have? How would you behave? What kind of environment would you work in? Would you need additional education?

The mission is always to achieve the vision. Assuming that you can define "world-class project manager," you can declare that as your mission.

Assessing Yourself

Assessing your developmental needs is important before you continue. You know what you want to achieve, but what do you need to do to accomplish the goal? Once you have a clear vision—which defines your skill set requirements and other attributes—you must determine where you must be when you are finished, and then decide where you are right now. Any gap between where you are and where you want to be represents a developmental need.

This can be done in a complicated or a simple way. The complicated approach would be to have a job counseling service give you a number of assessment tests. The simple approach is to identify the requisite skills, then rate your present capability on a scale of 1 to 5, together with your desired future capability. You can also use Bob Wysocki's web site to determine areas in which you need to develop skills, whatever your overall approach to getting there may later turn out to be.

Get Involved in PMI®

The Project Management Institute (PMI) is the professional association for project managers. As of April 2003, they have 100,000 members, and growth is so exponential that this number will probably be grossly in error by the time this book reaches you. PMI publishes a monthly magazine, a quarterly journal, has local chapters in most large cities, and holds an annual conference that is attended by several thousand people. Networking with your peers is one of the best ways to learn the requirements of the profession and get valuable ideas on how to advance your career. It can also be the source of job leads.

Getting Your PMP®

If you do join PMI, you may also want to get your Project Manager Professional (PMP) designation. This is accomplished by passing an exam administered by PMI and submitting evidence that you have logged the required hours of work experience. You can't just pass the exam to get certified—PMI requires that you have work experience as well, so that the PMP certifies you are actually qualified to manage projects. A number of study guides are available to help you pass the test, including one in this McGraw-Hill series by Bob Dudley and myself (Dudley & Lewis, 2003, in progress).

2. DEVELOP A STRATEGY

Strategy is an overall game plan for achieving your mission. As an example of this, you might decide to accept a job with an organization that has an active professional development program, one in which mentoring of employees is common. Or you may decide that you are going to get a Master's in Project Management, so that you have excellent qualifications for the job.

Either way, this is your strategy. Once you have defined it, you can turn to developing tactics or an implementation plan.

3. DEVELOP AN IMPLEMENTATION PLAN

Your implementation plan defines the specific activities in which you will engage to achieve your strategy. Will you get into a Master's program that allows you to go part-time? Or one that is on-line? If part-time, how many courses will you take each semester? How will you fund your program? What kind of timelines are involved? You need to answer all of these questions in order to develop a good plan, just as you would in any project.

4. EXECUTION AND CONTROL

Once you have an implementation plan, you can execute it. Assuming that you have time-sequenced activities in the plan, you can monitor your progress toward achieving task outcomes. You may have to make "course" corrections, due to unforeseen events that derail some part of your plan. The death of a relative, the birth of a child, a change in job responsibilities (such as a heavy increase in travel, which makes it difficult for you to attend classes)—all of these can require changes to your original plan. The important thing is to revise your plan, not just abandon it. Any goal worth having will require some sacrifice.

5. CLOSE OUT AND CELEBRATE!

Congratulations! You're a world-class project manager! All project completions should be celebrated. Be sure to do a lessons-learned review before the final closeout. Ask yourself what you did well and what you would do better if you did it all over again.

References and Reading List

Adams, John D. (Editor) *Transforming Leadership: from Vision to Results.* Alexandria, VA: Miles River Press, 1986.

Ailes, Roger. *You Are the Message: Secrets of the Master Communicators.* Homewood, IL: Dow Jones-Irwin, 1988.

Albrecht, Karl. *The Northbound Train.* New York: AMACOM, 1994.

Argyris, Chris. *Overcoming Organizational Defenses: Facilitating Organizational Learning.* Boston: Allyn and Bacon, 1990.

Barker, Joel A. *Future Edge.* New York: William Morrow, 1992.

Barker, Joel A. *Wealth, Innovation & Diversity.* Videotape. Carlsbad, CA: CRM Learning, 2000.

Bennis, Warren G. *Managing the Dream: Reflections on Leadership and Change.* Cambridge, MA: Perseus, 2000.

Bennis, Warren G., and Nanus, Burt. *Leaders: The Strategies for Taking Charge.* New York: Harper & Row, 1985.

Brooks, F. P. *The Mythical Man-Month: Essays on Software Engineering.* Reading, MA: Addison-Wesley, 1975.

Bunker, Barbara Benedict, and Billie T. Alban. *Large Group Interventions: Engaging the Whole System for Rapid Change.* San Francisco: Jossey-Bass, 1997.

Burns, James McGregor. *Leadership.* New York: Harper & Row, 1978.

Buzan, Tony. *The Mind Map Book.* New York: NAL/Dutton, 1996.

Chen, Yanping, and Francis N. Arko. *Principles of Contracting for Project Management.* Arlington, VA: UMT Press, 2003

Cialdini, Robert B. *Influence: The Power of Persuasion, Revised Edition.* New York: Quill, 1993.

133

Covey, Stephen. *The 7 Habits of Highly Effective People.* New York: Fireside Books, 1989.

Deming, Edwards. *Out of the Crisis.* Cambridge, MA: Massachusetts Institute of Technology, 1986.

Drucker, Peter F. *Management: Tasks, Responsibilities, Practices.* New York: Harper & Row, 1973, 1974.

Dudley, Robert, and James P. Lewis. *Preparing for the PMP Exam.* New York: McGraw-Hill, 2003.

Dyer, Wayne. *You'll See It When You Believe It.* New York: Avon Books, 1989.

Fleming, Quentin W., and Koppelman, Joel M. *Earned Value Project Management.* Upper Darbey, PA: Project Management Institute, 1996.

Frame, J. Davidson. *Managing Projects in Organizations.* San Francisco: Jossey-Bass, 1995.

Frame, J. Davidson. *The New Project Management,* Second Edition. San Francisco: Jossey-Bass, 2002.

Frame, J. Davidson. *Project Finance: Tools and Techniques.* Arlington, VA: UMT Press, 2003.

Frankl, Viktor. *Man's Search for Meaning,* Third Edition. New York: Touchstone, 1984.

Gause, Donald, and Gerald Weinberg. *Exploring Requirements: Quality Before Design.* New York: Dorset House Publishing, 1989.

Gawain, Shakti. *Creative Visualization.* Novato, CA: New World Library, 2002.

Graham, Robert J. and Englund, Randall L. *Creating an Environment for Successful Projects.* San Francisco: Jossey-Bass, 1997.

Harvey, Jerry B. *The Abilene Paradox: and Other Meditations on Management.* San Diego: University Associates, 1988.

Heller, Robert. *Achieving Excellence.* New York: DK Publishing, 1999.

Heller, Robert, and Hindle, Tim. *Essential Manager's Manual.* New York: DK Publishing, 1998.

Herrmann, Ned. *The Creative Brain.* Lake Lure, NC: Brain Books, 1995.

Herrmann, Ned. *The Whole Brain Business Book.* New York: McGraw-Hill, 1996.

Hersey, Paul, and Blanchard, Kenneth. *Management of Organizational Behavior: Utilizing Human Resources,* Fourth Edition. Englewood Cliffs, NJ: Prentice-Hall, 1981.

Johnson, Spencer. *Who Moved My Cheese?* New York: G. P. Putnam's Sons, 2002.

Kayser, Tom. *Mining Group Gold.* New York: McGraw-Hill, 1995.

Keirsey, David. *Please Understand Me II.* Del Mar, CA: Prometheus Nemesis Book Company, 1998.

Kouzes, James M., and Posner, Barry Z. *The Leadership Challenge: How to Get Extraordinary Things Done in Organizations.* San Francisco: Jossey-Bass, 1987.

Leider, Richard J. *Life Skills: Taking Charge of Your Personal and Professional Growth.* Paramus, NJ: Prentice Hall, 1994.

Leider, Richard J. *The Power of Purpose: Creating Meaning in Your Life and Work.* San Francisco: Berrett Koehler, 1997.

Lewis, James. *Fundamentals of Project Management.* New York: AMACOM, 1993.

Lewis, James. *Mastering Project Management.* New York: McGraw-Hill, 1998.

Lewis, James. *The Project Manager's Desk Reference,* Second Edition. New York: McGraw-Hill, 2000.

Lewis, James. *Team-Based Project Management.* New York: AMACOM, 1997.

McClelland, David. *Power: The Inner Experience.* New York: Halsted Press, 1975.

McGraw, Phillip. *Life Strategies: Doing What Works, Doing What Matters.* New York, Hyperion, 1999.

Michaelson, Gerald A. *Sun Tzu, The Art of War for Managers, 50 Strategic Rules.* Avon, MA: Adams Media Corporation, 2001.

Mintzberg, Henry. *Mintzberg on Management.* New York: The Free Press, 1989.

Morrison, Terri; Conaway, Wayne A.; and Borden, George A. *Kiss, Bow or Shake Hands.* Avon, MA: Adams Media Corporation, 1994.

NASA. *100 Rules for Project Managers.*

Packard, Vance. *The Pyramid Climbers.* New York: McGraw-Hill, 1962.

Page, Rick. *Hope Is Not a Strategy.* New York: Nautilus Press, 2002.

Patterson, Marvin. *Accelerating Innovation: Improving the Processes of Product Development.* New York: Van Nostrand Reinhold, 1993.

Peters, Tom. *Liberation Management.* New York: Knopf, 1992.

Peters, Tom. *Thriving on Chaos*. New York: Knopf, 1987.

Peters, Tom. "The WOW Project." *Fast Company* magazine, May 1999.

Peters, Tom, and Bob Waterman. *In Search of Excellence: Lessons from America's Best-Run Companies*. New York: Warner Books, 1988.

Rosen, Robert H. *Leading People: The 8 Proven Principles for Success in Business*. New York: Penguin Books, 1996.

Rosenthal, R., and Jacobson, L. *Pygmalion in the Classroom*. New Your: Holt, Rinehart, and Winston, 1968.

Sabbagh, Karl. *Twenty-First Century Jet*. New York: Scribner, 1996.

Smith, Hyrum W. *The 10 Natural Laws of Successful Time and Life Management*. New York: Warner Books, 1994.

Smith, Preston G., and Reinertsen, Donald G. *Developing Products in Half the Time*. New York: Van Nostrand, 1995.

Sugimoto, T. *Estimation On the Project Management Workload*. In "Proceedings of the International Conference on Project Management," Singapore, July 31 to August 2, 2002.

Sykes, Charles. *A Nation of Victims: The Decay of the American Character*. New York: St. Martin's Press, 1992.

Sykes, Charles. *Dumbing Down Our Kids*. New York: St. Martin's Press, 1995.

Wheatley, Margaret. *Leadership and New Science*. San Francisco: Berrett-Koehler, 1992.

Wysocki, Robert K. *Effective Project Management*, Second Edition. New York: Wiley, 2000.

Wysocki, Robert K, and Lewis, James P. *The World-Class Project Manager*. Boston: Perseus Books, 2001.

Index

About the Author

J*ames P. Lewis, Ph.D.*, is an experienced project manager who now teaches seminars on the subject throughout the United States, England, and the Far East. His solid, no-nonsense approach is largely the result of the 15 years he spent in industry, working as an electrical engineer, engaged in the design and development of communication equipment. He held various positions, including Project Manager, Product Engineering Manager, and Chief Engineer, for Aerotron, Inc., and ITT Telecommunications, both of Raleigh, NC. He also was a Quality Manager for ITT Telecom, managing a department of 63 quality engineers, line inspectors, and test technicians.

While he was an engineering manager, he began working on a doctorate in organizational psychology because of his conviction that a manager can only succeed by developing good interpersonal skills.

Since 1980, Dr. Lewis has trained over 25,000 supervisors and managers in Argentina, Canada, England, Germany, India, Indonesia, Malaysia, Mexico, Singapore, Sweden, Thailand, and the United States. He has written articles for *Training and Development Journal, Apparel Industry* magazine, and *Transportation and Distribution* magazine. He is the author of *Project Planning, Scheduling and Control*, Third Edition; *Mastering Project Management; The Project*

147

Manager's Desk Reference; Working Together: 12 Principles for Achieving Excellence in Managing Projects, Teams, and Organizations; and *Project Leadership,* published by McGraw-Hill; as well as *Fundamentals of Project Management: Developing Core Competencies to Help Outperform the Competition,* Second Edition; *How to Build and Manage a Winning Project Team;* and *Team-Based Project Management,* published by the American Management Association. He is co-author, with Bob Wysocki, of *The World-Class Project Manager: A Professional Development Guide,* published by Perseus in 2001. The first edition of *Project Planning, Scheduling and Control* has been published in a Spanish edition, and the AMACOM book *Fundamentals of Project Management* has been published in Portuguese and Latvian. Several of his books have also been published in Chinese, and *Project Leadership* is being translated into Spanish and Russian.

He has a B.S. in Electrical Engineering and a Ph.D. in Psychology, both from NC State University in Raleigh. He is a member of the Project Management Institute. He is also a certified Herrmann Brain Dominance Instrument practitioner.

He is president of The Lewis Institute, Inc., a training and consulting company specializing in project management, which he founded in 1981.

Jim is married to the former Lea Ann McDowell, and they live in Vinton, Virginia.